# DEALING
# WITH
# DIFFICULT
# RELATIVES AND
# IN-LAWS

*How to deal with angry, demanding and manipulative
relatives and in-laws*

**REVISED EDITION**

**ROBERTA CAVA**

Published by Cava Consulting
info@dealingwithdifficultpeople.info
www.dealingwithdifficultpeople.info

**Cava, Roberta**

**Dealing with Difficult Relatives & In-laws**

*How to deal with angry, demanding and manipulative Relatives and In-laws*

**REVISED EDITION**

National Library of Australia

Cataloguing-in-publication data:

ISBN: 978-0-9872594-8-6

## BOOKS BY ROBERTA CAVA
# Non-Fiction

Dealing with Difficult People (23 publishers – in 17 languages)
Dealing with Difficult Situations – at Work and at Home
Dealing with Difficult Spouses and Children
Dealing with Difficult Relatives and In-Laws
Dealing with Domestic Violence and Child Abuse
Dealing with School Bullying
Dealing with Workplace Bullying
Retirement Village Bullies
Keeping Our Children Safe
Just say no
What am I going to do with the rest of my life?
Before tying the knot – Questions couples Must ask each other Before they marry!
How Women can advance in business
Survival Skills for Supervisors and Managers
Human Resources at its Best!
Human Resources Policies and Procedures - Australia
Employee Handbook
Easy Come – Hard to go – The Art of Hiring, Disciplining and Firing Employees
Time and Stress – Today's silent killers
Take Command of your Future – Make things Happen
Belly Laughs for All! – Volumes 1 to 6
Wisdom of the World! The happy, sad and wise things in life!

### Fiction

That Something Special
Something Missing
Trilogy: Life Gets Complicated
Life Goes On
Life Gets Better

# ACKNOWLEDGEMENTS

My gratitude is extended to the thousands of participants of my seminars who contributed ideas on how *they* handled their difficult siblings, relatives, parents and seniors.

Also, sincere thanks go to the Canadian Mental Health Association who allowed me to quote directly from one of their information booklets.

# DEALING WITH DIFFICULT RELATIVES & IN-LAWS

*By Roberta Cava*

## INTRODUCTION

## CHAPTER 1 - EVALUATE YOUR ACTIONS

* Controlling your moods
* One of 'those" days
* Handling your emotions
* How to "Keep your Cool"
* Using logic and emotion
* Sample situations
  - dealing with others' anger
  - dealing with your anger
  - handling guilty feelings
  - handling revengeful feelings
  - feeling stressed
  - feeling depressed
  - if only... I should have…
* Changing your reactions
* Comfort zones
* What's important
* How are you spending your life right now?
* Unwarranted or unnecessary criticism
* Jumping to conclusions
* Truly Incorrigibly difficult people
* Rehearsals

## CHAPTER 2 - WHAT KIND OF PERSON ARE YOU?

* Personality types
  - Strengths, weaknesses, positive and negative points
* How you get along with other personality types
* Manipulation
* How your behaviour affects others
* Behaviour Styles: passive, aggressive, assertive, passive resistant, indirect aggressive, and passive/aggressive behaviours
* Behaviour in traditional roles
* Worry
* Lethargic, apathetic and unhappy?

## CHAPTER 3 - COMMUNICATION SKILLS FOR DEALING WITH DIFFICULT PEOPLE

* Same words - different meanings
* Skill of paraphrasing
* Skill of feedback
  - process of feedback
  - feedback steps
* Skill of listening
  - kinds of bad listeners
  - blocks to effective listening
* Non-verbal communication
    -space bubbles
    -eye contact
    -lying
* How you appear to others
* Interrupters
* Stuck record technique
* Teasing

## CHAPTER 4 - DIFFICULT SIBLINGS

* Sibling rivalry
* Personality differences
* Friends who smoke
* Procrastinator
    -hurry-up type
    -I'll decide tomorrow
* Forgetful
* Common-Law Marriage
* Sloppy Brother
* No privacy
* Morning - night people
* Chronic Fatigue Syndrome
* No time for ME
* Expects favours
* Borrowing money
* Tantrums
* *"Aggressive female"* label
* Poor listener
* Repetitive phrases
* Mumbler

## CHAPTER 5 - DIFFICULT RELATIVES

# BIBLIOGRAPHY

# INTRODUCTION

This publication is a sequel to my internationally best-selling book *Dealing with Difficult People* that has been so popular since its release in 1990 that the publishers released revised editions in 2000, 2004, 2008, 2013 and 2014 and is now available through twenty-two publishers and in sixteen languages. Sequels to that book are: *Dealing with Difficult Spouses and Children; Dealing with Difficult Situations - At Work and at Home; Dealing with Domestic Violence and Child Abuse; Dealing with School Bullying; Dealing with Workplace Bullying and Retirement Village Bullies.*

Rather than gearing this book towards those in the workforce, I've slanted it towards siblings, parents, relatives, seniors and in-laws who may be, upset, irate, rude, impatient, emotional, persistent or just plain aggressive.

These difficult people may try to manipulate you into doing things you don't want to do, keep you from doing the things you want to do, try to give you negative feelings about yourself or make you lose your cool.

This book is not a cure and I'm not presumptuous enough to think I have all the answers. What you will gain however, are alternatives to the way you're presently dealing with problems; to give you the option of trying plan 'B' and 'C' when your plan 'A' doesn't work.

Have you started your morning feeling happy with the world, but find your day going rapidly downhill because of the difficult situations you encounter? Do you let other people or situations control what kind of day you have? Do you often feel as if you are not in control during difficult situations? It's the little annoyances that can ruin your day, so if you can handle them constructively, you're certainly ahead of the game.

Learning to deal with difficult people involves learning how to manage your side of a two-way transaction. This gives the other person a chance to work with you to resolve whatever is making him or her difficult. Although you might make several attempts to change other's difficult behaviour - your chance of making a difference depends upon the receptiveness of your difficult people to change. What you do have full control over however - is your reaction to others' difficult behaviour.

Difficult people are the ones who try to:

- Make us lose our cool;
- Force us to do things we don't want to do;

- Prevent us from doing what we want or need to do;
- Often use coercion, manipulation or other underhanded methods to get their way;
- Make us do their share of the work.
- Make us feel guilty if we don't go along with their wishes;
- Make us feel anxious, upset, frustrated, angry, depressed, jealous, inferior, defeated, sad or any other negative feeling; or

People come in all shapes and sizes and they also display many kinds of behaviour. Many use manipulation to get their way, using passive-resistant, passive/aggressive, indirect aggressive and aggressive behaviours. What tactics do you use when trying to persuade someone to do something? Do you try to manipulate others by using negative manipulation?

Could others object to this manipulation that results in many of the difficult situations you face? As you read the examples in this book ask yourself if you too could be guilty of any of the situations that cause such grief to others.

What will you gain by reading this book? You'll learn techniques that will enable you to remain calm, gain a more positive attitude and maintain your emotional well being when faced with life's negative situations. Your self-confidence level will rise, and you'll be in control when dealing with difficult spouses, relatives and in-laws.

How do I know the techniques identified in this book really work? More than 55,000 participants (internationally) who have attended my *Dealing with Difficult People* seminars endorse the techniques described in this book and use them often.

# CHAPTER 1

# EVALUATE YOUR ACTIONS

### *Controlling your moods:*

Before you can tackle difficult relatives and in-laws, it's essential that you have *your* act together. Could your actions or behaviour be a trigger for the other person's difficult behaviour? Could you have done or said something that started the difficult encounter?

Perhaps you're a moody person yourself? Do you have mood swings that affect what kind of day you have? Are you up one hour, down the next - up one day, down the next? If you're normally a moody person, you've probably allowed others' behaviour and actions to affect your day.

If you believe that outside circumstances cause unhappiness and that you have no control over this unhappiness - you're wrong. Outside forces and events cannot be harmful unless *you allow them to affect you.* Happiness comes largely from within a person. While external events may irritate or annoy you, you still have control over how you respond.

Every day we're faced with negative situations that cause negative emotions. Some emotions they initiate make us feel:

Angry; embarrassed; dumb; hurt; intimidated; suspicious; guilty; rejected; troubled; anxious; nervous; uneasy; depressed; distressed; tense; frustrated; concerned; upset; ignored; flustered; emotional; disappointed; humiliated; worried; ashamed; resentful; agitated; jealous; restricted; remorseful; inferior; stupid; offended; insecure; sad; or hindered.

Is there any wonder why many people have become negative-thinking people? So, watch for the physical signs (which you will likely have when faced with people trying to make you feel any of the above) and ask yourself whether you're overreacting. If you've determined that the feeling is not realistic, you've overreacted. This could be ten minutes after the negative situation happened. Turn off your negative reaction - let it go! If you find your mind constantly returning to these negative situations, remind yourself that you're giving someone else control over your life - and don't do it!

How many of these negative feelings have you **not** felt within the past month? Is there any wonder that you're stressed out with so many negatives bombarding you every day?

When faced with these negative emotions, most of us react automatically - the way we always have - whether it's good or bad. For instance, when someone throws a cutting remark your way or makes an angry comment - do you keep your equilibrium and handle the barbs in a positive way? How about situations where someone is trying to make you feel guilty about something? Can you maintain your composure and keep control over your emotions and reactions under those circumstances? Or do you react almost automatically to the negative stimulus from others and retaliate, feel hurt or guilty?

What happens to your self-esteem level when you're not in control of situations? Does it stay intact or is it bruised by the other person's negative actions? This is what can keep you off-balance. When you're able to control your emotions and reactions when faced with difficult situations, you also retain your feeling of self-worth. When you feel in control of situations, your feet stay firmly planted. But, if you react badly to someone's negative behaviour, you may find yourself losing that control.

Do you blame others for how you feel? When you make comments such as, *'She makes me so mad when she...'* Or, *'He always makes me feel so inferior.'* Or, your own self-talk says, *'You goofed again. How dumb can you be? Won't you ever learn?'* you're allowing others (and yourself) to ruin your day. By allowing yourself to feel badly about situations or take on guilt you don't deserve, you're giving *yourself* a bad day. Let's face it - you're not going to gain anything by blaming others for the way you feel. Remember,

- *You* decide whether someone's angry remark will upset you or not.
- *You* allow yourself to feel hurt when someone speaks uncaring words to you and
- *You* choose to feel guilty, even if the feeling is not warranted.

You relinquish an important part of your self-esteem, if you allow others to govern whether you have a good or bad day.

How can you stop this from happening? You simply turn negative situations off and don't let them affect you emotionally. If you allow yourself to absorb the negative feeling, it's got to get out somehow, so you pass it on to someone else.' Because you've probably been on *"automatic pilot"* when reacting to negative situations in the past, this technique may take considerable practice - but it's worth it!

### One of those days

I'm sure you've faced a day where everything seems to go wrong! In fact, you wish you could go back to bed (and it's only 10:00 am!) How you react to this kind of day often determines the outcome of it. Most people respond by saying, *'Oh boy. It's going to be one of those days!'* They expect the rest of the day to be terrible - and of course it is! They set themselves up for a bad day and are rewarded accordingly.

If you find yourself facing the kind of day where three or four negative situations occur - have a talk with yourself. Instead of saying *'It's going to be one of those days!'* say, *'Thank goodness I got that out of the way!'* What you're doing is telling yourself that the rest of the day is going to be better (because all the really bad stuff has already happened)! Try changing your attitude from negative to positive when you're having a bad day and see if your day doesn't turn around.

### Handling your emotions

When others become irate, rude, impatient or angry, you probably become upset yourself. The first step towards keeping your cool - is to change your response. My life changed when I realised I could choose how I reacted when faced with difficult situations. I could either *take* the bad feelings thrust upon me by others or simply *not take* them. I accomplished this by stopping my defense mechanism from kicking in. This is the same defensive system that cavemen and cavewomen had. They prepared themselves mentally and physically to either stand and fight the dinosaur or run like crazy in the opposite direction.

Today, the same reaction occurs when we're faced with dangerous or negative situations. Stop for a moment and ask yourself how you react mentally and physically when someone's angry with you, has hurt you with his/her comments or has tried to make you feel guilty about something. Often, your fight or flight mechanism kicks in and you'll likely have some of the following symptoms:

- rapid pulse
- increased perspiration

- pounding heart
- blood pressure rises
- faster breathing
- tensing of leg and arm muscles
- nervous stomach
- tightened stomach muscles
- head and stomach aches
- loss of or increased appetite
- digestion slows down
- rashes and hives
- gritting of teeth
- clenching of the jaw
- clammy feeling
- extremities cold
- body trembles
- inability to sit still
- raging thoughts
- excessively gripping emotions
- impatience
- become jumpy
- emotional
- insomnia

The first step I took towards becoming more immune to others' barbs and difficult behaviour was to know when my defence mechanism kicked in. I recognised that I was mentally and physically preparing to defend myself. My reactions were - my heart pounded, my thoughts raced, I'd feel the blood rushing to my face and my muscles would stiffen (mostly my stomach muscles). Do you have similar reactions? Analyse what your fight or flight reactions are when you face difficult situations.

As soon as I identify this reaction in myself, I stop (this takes only a split second) and question whether I'm reacting correctly to the negative situation. Nine times out of ten, I recognise that I'm over-reacting or am allowing *myself* to feel badly.

I also recognise that my self-esteem is lower when I face situations where I don't feel *"in control"*. I feel incompetent when I am in the throes of difficult situations. When I learned how to control my reactions, I could maintain a high self-esteem level. This allowed me to direct my energy towards positive, rather than negative use.

Instead of running away, feeling hurt or defending myself - I dealt with the situation. When I learned this simple technique, I found I had far more control over my everyday moods. Gone were the roller-coaster mood swings of the past. Other people didn't decide what kind of day I'd have - I did! You too can have this control. The ability to master this skill is easier than you might believe. All it takes is practice - but you *can* do it! As soon as you feel the need to defend yourself - stop and practice my technique.

If you don't turn off your defense mechanism, you'll allow others to give you their negative feelings. If you allow negative feelings to go in, they rumble around, but must be released somehow. And how do you release these feelings? You give them to someone or something else. You yell back at the person giving you the bad feeling, are nasty to the next person you see, you kick the dog or even throw something.

Sound familiar? Why are you allowing someone else to trigger these responses? Remember, you can't control other people's behaviour, but you *can* control how you respond to their behaviour. By accepting their anger, you've given them control over the next few minutes, hours or even days of your life. Is this person worthy of having this much control over your emotions? In most instances, I think you'll decide a definite, *no*.

Of course, there will be exceptions where this technique won't work because the situations are serious:

* Having an accident or being seriously ill;
* Getting fired from your job unjustly; or
* Someone you know is seriously ill or dying.

But these are exceptions. Most everyday moods and reactions you *can* control.

### How to 'keep your cool'

Think of a situation where a family member is obviously in a bad mood. Instead of realizing that they're not going to be easy to talk to - you forge ahead and respond negatively to their actions. You allow their comments to affect you and end up with hurt feelings on both sides.

Why did you allow this to happen? Later the person will likely apologize to you for his/her behaviour. Watch your timing. Anticipate the other person's responses and don't push them, especially if the timing is wrong. Don't allow the person's angry comments to affect you and affect a good relationship.

However, if this person is in a bad mood most of the time, you shouldn't have to *"walk on eggs"* and watch every word you say when talking with them. If this is the case, confront the person and explain your feelings about his/her behaviour using the feedback technique (see Chapter 3).

Keeping your cool when you're under pressure takes concentrated effort. If you're quick to become angry - focus your energies on stopping your automatic defense mechanism and instead, try the following tactics:

Tune into your feelings. I feel sad ... unhappy ... angry ...

Narrow down or find the cause of your feelings. Did the person go back on his or her word? Did s/he let you down or break a trust? Try to understand why you feel angry, sad, unhappy, fearful etc. Did s/he accuse you unfairly or did you deserve his or her reaction because of something you did or did not do?

Deal with your feelings realistically and share your feelings with the person who upset you. Communicate - don't shut them out. For instance, say, *'When you yell at me, I freeze up and can't respond the way I want to.'*

Take a walk. Use your adrenalin effectively by aiming your energy towards constructive activities. Determine why s/he did or said what s/he did. How should you deal with his or her actions? What could you say or do that would resolve the problem? Then do it.

### Using logic and emotion

These two forces - logic and emotion, are at work throughout our lives. They're often pushing and pulling in opposite directions. The prevailing one may determine how we get along with others and can affect our level of achievement.

As children, we may have very pleasant memories and remember feeling pleasure, happiness, excitement and fun and love (all positive emotions). Or we may have very negative memories; feel insecure and inferior when our achievements were compared to others. Our school grades, our prowess at sports and our physical appearance were all carefully evaluated. This often resulted in negative behaviour such as pouting, tantrums, shouting, arguing, cursing and blaming others, spreading gossip, giving the silent treatment, showing jealousy or resentment.

These negative responses seldom received favourable reactions. As most of us matured, we learned to evaluate our behaviour and questioned the validity of others' comments or behaviour.

### *Sample Situations:*

Here are examples of how you could be going on *"automatic pilot"* when facing negative situations:

### 1. *You* allow yourself to accept others' anger

For example: You've been shopping and return to your car to find that someone has put a dent in the side of your car door. The parking spot beside your car is empty, so the driver has left without dealing with the damage. You're furious, get in your car and squeal out of the parking lot. After you phone your insurance agent, you contact all your close friends and rant and rave about the damage done to your car.

How long do you stay mad at the driver of the other car? And what good does it do? I've seen people stay at a fever pitch for hours relating their story to others. They say, *'Do you know what happened to me when I was shopping this morning? Some dumb person whammed their car door into mine and there's a big dent in my passenger door!'*

When you noticed the dent in your car, you had two choices:

- Stay upset about it.
- Handle the situation by:
  (i) reporting the incident to your insurance company,
  (ii) getting your car fixed and forgetting about the situation.

Your anger will have *no* effect on the driver who damaged your car. In the first situation, you *chose* to remain upset. You can't blame the other driver for your continued anger.

9

## 2. *You* respond negatively to guilt

Sadly, we live in a guilt-ridden society where we allow others to make us feel guilty and we're very efficient at giving ourselves guilt feelings as well. We feel guilty if we can't understand what someone's saying, or we feel guilty because we make mistakes. Identify things you've done in the past that you're not proud of. Instead of wallowing in guilt, learn from the experience. If an apology is needed to remove the guilt - then apologize.

### a) *Others throw guilt at you, so* you *allow yourself to feel guilty:*

Our parents are often the ones who can give us the most effective and guilt-laden feelings. You can't change the past despite how you or they feel about it. Some parents have long memories and bring up events that happened years ago.

When others try to make you feel guilty, stop and identify what their comments really mean. Analyze whether there's any truth to their comments - then act accordingly. Recognise when others are manipulating you by trying to make you feel guilty. Accept that you have the right to choose to do or be something other than what others may expect or want you to be.

For instance, insisting that there's no other profession worthwhile other than nursing (when you want to be a social worker). It's nice to have your parent's approval, but not at the risk of your feeling of self-worth. You have the right to choose how you live (providing you're not breaking the laws of the land). You also must be ready to take the consequences of your behaviour and choices. Recognise that others (your children perhaps?) have this right as well. It's unfair to force your ideas on others by trying to make the person feel guilty.

Others may try to transfer their responsibility to you or try to obtain pity from you. By attempting to make you feel guilty, they make comments such as:

> '*I spent all day cooking this meal and it takes you fifteen minutes to eat it. The least you could do is help clear the table!*'
> '*You never call me any more.*'
> '*If you loved me, you'd...*'
> '*What will the neighbors think?*'
> '*How can you just sit there watching your stupid football game when there's so much to do around here?*'

How do you handle a person who's trying to make you feel guilty? First, identify whether their comments or statements are true. If so, deal with the issue. If the guilt is not warranted, try to establish why they're trying to manipulate you and what they expect to gain by doing so.

For example: You've worked very hard painting the bathroom and are very proud of your accomplishment. You wait patiently for recognition from members of your family. Is recognition likely to come? Typically - it isn't. What you're more likely to hear about, is a small portion of the task you did incorrectly. *'You missed this spot.'* Or, *'The paint ran here.'*

Unfortunately, if someone criticizes you, you may automatically accept his or her comments without question. This allows the one giving criticism to you, to control how you feel about yourself and/or your work. This obviously can seriously affect your self-confidence level. Then you may get the feeling that you *did* do a poor job and accept the guilt feelings that accompany the criticism.

Learn to evaluate the relevancy of other people's comments. Are your guilt feelings warranted? Could you be responding negatively because that's the way you've always responded in the past? Re-evaluate the situation. What type of job do you feel you did? Were you originally pleased? Why aren't you pleased now?

Don't count on others to give recognition. If they do give recognition - think of their praise as *"gravy."* But you don't need gravy on the potatoes every night, do you? Like too much gravy (which can make you swell up) you could become swellheaded if you received praise for everything you did.

Never compete against the record of someone else. Just work to improve your record of accomplishments. The person you should be trying to please is *you.* Most of us set high standards for ourselves. When you feel you're being shoved around psychologically, state how you feel (no apologies). The fact that others disapprove of what you do has nothing to do with what or who you are. You're not responsible for the happiness of others - that's their responsibility. You're accountable only for your own emotions.

### b) *You make yourself feel guilty:*

As if others' criticism isn't bad enough, we all seem to have a little twerp inside us who loves to criticise. This voice makes such comments as, *'You goofed again! Can't you do anything right?'* If you've given a situation your best effort – that's all you can expect of yourself. For some reason society has taught us to feel guilty if we make mistakes.

If you made a mistake - recognise that it's just that - a mistake - and simply don't do it again. Mistakes are to learn from and should not make us feel as if we're failures. Stop being hypercritical and start giving yourself positive reinforcement. If you've done a good job, mentally pat yourself on the back with such thoughts as, *'I'm really proud of how well I painted that room.'* Then give yourself some small reward.

### 3. *You* allow yourself to have revengeful feelings

Think of a time when someone's *"done you wrong"*. Did you fuss and fume - vowing to make them pay for their actions? How long did it take you to plan your revenge and follow it through to completion? Did you spend years planning revenge for a perceived wrongdoing, and did that hate overshadow just about everything else in your life?

A prime example is a divorced spouse who is, *'Going to pay him or her back for what s/he's done to me!'* These individuals have difficulty getting on with their lives, because they're so caught up in their revengeful thoughts. Some waste precious years and other romantic relationships instead of getting on with their lives.

Stand back from the situation for a moment and analyse what happened during the time you were planning your revenge. Who had control over your time, emotions and energy while you were planning your revenge? Concentrating on getting revenge, ties you to the wrongdoer - instead of allowing you to get on with your life!

If you find yourself having revengeful feelings and can deal with the issue right away - do so. But if you can't deal with the wrongdoer right away, drop the issue and don't allow thoughts of *"getting revenge"* to enter your mind. Remind yourself, that if you're dwelling on the other person's negative acts, you're still giving him or her control over your life. Is that person worthy of having that kind of impact on your life? I doubt it!

It's not easy to turn off feelings of revenge and you may feel you're being unfair to yourself by letting others off the hook too easily. If you've had a feud with someone, do you wait for *him or her* to do something to mend the rift or feel *they* should pay for their wrongdoings? Often, forgiving is the only action that can mend and heal. You might say, *'Your sister didn't gossip behind your back and pass on untrue information about you.'*

It's ironic, but the saying *'What comes around - goes around,'* is true. You just need to stand back and watch it happen. This takes faith on your part – but think of the benefits. No longer will you be giving the other person control over your life.

### 4. *You* allow yourself to feel stressed

We may find ourselves feeling stressed when we face an overload of work. If we can't handle our time properly, it makes us more stressed. The more stressed we become, the more trouble we have dealing with our difficult people and situations.

If this is your problem, eliminate some of your stress. Take a time management course or read time management books to help you choose priorities. Spend time on *your* priorities. Make *"To Do"* lists, so you'll know exactly how many tasks you can handle in a day. This enables you to focus completely on the task you're completing at that moment, instead of being distracted by those that are waiting to be done.

### 5. *You* allow yourself to feel depressed

Normally, some important loss triggers depression. You may feel despondent when you lose items of value, friends, health, promotions, income or your value as a human being. As you mature, you'll lose many items of value - jobs, income, prestige, friends and health. You may be in a home situation that's not suitable. Your depression can be anger you turn against yourself because you may feel helpless to do anything to change your situation.

Or, you may allow yourself to feel depressed for no other reason except that it's Monday morning. You find yourself energized Friday afternoon, but feel down or depressed Monday morning. It's possible that you may be one of the eight out of ten people who are in the wrong type of employment. These statistics might appear high, but if you conduct your own survey, you'll likely confirm that it's true.

Ask people if they feel they're in the right job for them or are there other tasks they'd rather be doing. Ask yourself that question too. If you said you're in the wrong job, you may have to find more suitable employment. After all, you likely spend about ten hours a day, five days a week getting ready for, travelling to or working at your job. The average man spends forty-five years of his adult life in the workplace and women aren't far behind with thirty-five years in the workplace (I said the workplace – not the volunteer work she does at home!)

Isn't it worth the effort to find out what kind of job you'd be happy in? Or is it easier to stay in your rut? Having control over your life is a necessity for lifelong happiness. Allow yourself that control and you'll allow yourself to have a happier, healthier and more positive life.

**6. *You* use such phrases as 'If only...' Or 'I should have...'**

There are many cop-out phrases you may be using to bind yourself to the past. Do you find yourself using phrases such as?

> *'If only I were younger, slimmer, more attractive...'*
> *'I should have done this years ago.'*
> *'I should have been more careful.'*
> *'I was supposed to...'*
> *'I ought to...'*
> *'I have to...'*
> *'I must...'*
> *'I need to...'*
> *'I'm trying to...'*
> *'If you want me to...'*
> *'S/he made me...'*
> *'You always...'*
> *'You never...'*
> *'I'm this way because...'*
> *'I can't change the way I am because...'*
> *'The trouble with...' Or,*
> *'I can't...'*

Whenever possible, eliminate these phrases from your vocabulary unless you're willing to do something constructive about your comments. Remember that *you* choose to:

- Let others give you their anger;
- Let yourself become angry because someone put a dent in your car door or you got stuck in traffic;

14

- Feel guilty when you couldn't please others or because you made a mistake;
- Spend your valuable time on revengeful actions;
- Feel stressed when you face an overload of work;
- Feel depressed for no other reason than it's Monday morning; and/or
- Live in the past, using phrases such as *'If only...'* and *I should have...'*

### Changing your reactions

As soon as you notice the *"fight or flight"* reaction in yourself, stop and ask yourself these questions:

1. Am I reacting appropriately to this situation?
2. Should I really be having these negative feelings?
3. Could I be over-reacting?

If any of these are true, stop and vow that you won't allow these negative feelings to affect the next few minutes, hours, days or weeks of your life! You may find yourself ten minutes after a difficult situation in a full fight or flight mode. It's not too late to turn off your feelings and take control again. Bit by bit, you will decrease the time, until it becomes an almost automatic response.

### Comfort zones

When you choose a life style or decide to pursue a certain occupation, one of the criteria you should consider, is your comfort zone in the situation. The more comfort you have in a situation, the more likely you are to deal more favourably with the difficult people you meet.

Most people have different *"comfort zones"* in life, where they either feel comfortable or they don't. For some, speaking in front of a group of people would not take place in their *"comfort zone"*. Working with the public may or may not be in their *"comfort zone"*. Some may be more introverted and prefer to work alone, rather than with groups. Others may prefer detail-oriented positions rather than people-oriented ones. They may seek fast-paced occupations or are happier with more routine ones.

What are your low and high comfort zones? If you identify any glaring discrepancies between what you do every day and what you should be doing every day, you may have to make changes to your lifestyle.

### *What's important?*

Are you wandering through life with no specific goals? Are you in a rut? Are you existing, rather than living your life? If so, it's time to consider making some concrete goals so you have some direction to your life. Most of us would never just get in a car and drive if we were going on a journey. Instead, we would get out a map and learn where we were going. It always amazes me that people don't make a map of where their lives are heading. They wander through life allowing others and situations to determine where their life is headed. If this sounds like you, the following will likely interest you:

### 1. Your goals *must* be your own:

You're more likely to accomplish personal goals that you set for yourself than if you strive to achieve goals others want you to accomplish. This doesn't mean that you can't accept the goals of a spouse, friend or boss as your own. You can do this, but your motivation is going to be stronger if you consciously think through and talk through the advantages and disadvantages of working towards a goal - and make your own decision to pursue it. Knowledge of who we are and what we desire is essential - so we can establish goals based on our own internalised values.

### 2. Goals need to be clear, concrete - *and written down*

The purpose of writing goals is to clarify and make them concrete for you. Writing and revising goals forces you to make a commitment to yourself. Once written, you'll have more invested in the goal than before. Writing helps to keep the goal in front of you and reduces the possibility that it will be forgotten as new problems and new challenges appear.

It helps integrate your goals into projects and to identify conflicting goals. Make a contract and give a copy to a close friend or relative. It can also save you time, because part of the process involves determining the obstacles that will be in your way. You would determine how you would go over, under, around or through them to reach your goal. If there were too many obstacles, you may decide the goal is not reasonable or practical – but because you plotted it only on paper - you wouldn't have wasted the actual effort it may have taken, if you had tackled the goal itself.

### 3. Specific time deadlines aid in accomplishments of goals

Assigning target dates for completing each step of a plan provides constant reinforcement and a sense of accomplishment that helps sustain your motivation. Dates can and should be adjusted and changed, but make sure the excuses are authentic and they're not simply a way of procrastinating.

### 4. Start with short-range goals

Learning involves making mistakes as well as achieving success. Start your goal-setting by working on some short-range goals that are easily attainable. As these are accomplished, you'll gain more and more confidence in tackling more challenging long-range goals. Short-range goals are also more likely to be within your own control. Don't be concerned if the first statement of goals must be revised over and over - life is not stable - and things do change.

### 5. Consider legality, morality and ethics of your goals

Most people's value systems include a degree of concern for the legality, morality and ethics of their actions. You should consider these before you commit yourself to a goal.

### 6. Goals require realism and should be attainable

Having a goal is the first step to action, but if it is unrealistic or unattainable, it's not even a goal - but pure fantasy and daydreaming. The higher the goal; the stronger the motivation. But if you don't believe that accomplishment is possible, there's no motivation. If it feels right to you and if it makes sense to you and your respected friends; then it *is* possible.

### *How are you spending your life right now?*

What are you spending your valuable time doing right now? Are you putting the emphasis on doing things that are important to you? Or are you wasting much of your time doing things that aren't important or are not aiming you towards your life goals? If you're concerned about this, try the following time breakdown form - just for a week - and see how you really are spending your time.

There are 168 hours in a week. How did you spend your time within this past week? Make a graph with the following headings: Activity: Sunday; Monday; Tuesday etc. Under Activity put:

- Sleep
- Personal Hygiene (washing, hair care, makeup, shaving)
- Eating
- Travel (commuting)
- Work (salaried)
- Work (home)
- Pleasure (TV, sports, reading)
- Self Development (education, study)
- Illness

   **Total**

Then, decide how much time you spend at or with:

   *a. Working*
   *b. Family*
   *c. Social (community)*
   *d. Goof-off time or illness*

Inevitably, there will be days when you'll end up frustrated, with commitments stretching endlessly before you. Don't be ashamed to admit when you're in over your head. Perhaps you can delegate several of your responsibilities to another person (at least temporarily). If you find you're constantly working overtime, it's either: you have too many responsibilities or you're not using effective time management.

One couple found that they were not spending their time doing what they wanted to do. What they really wanted to do was travel but found they couldn't because they were chained to their home by their responsibilities. They'd had five children, so had a large home and lived in the country where they grew vegetables to save money for their large family. Because of the size of their home, the wife was kept very busy maintaining it and the husband had the yard, home repairs, the garden and the driveway to maintain.

However, their family had grown, and most had moved away. Their last child would be leaving for college the next month. Because of the distance of their home from the city, they both spent over an hour travelling to and from their jobs (2 hours each per work-day). They decided they'd sell their home in the country and move into a high-rise apartment in the city, so they'd be able to travel, as they wanted to. They then travelled only fifteen minutes each way to work and were able to close their apartment door and travel.

Another man wanted to get ahead in his career but didn't seem to have enough time to take the required additional courses in the evenings. After he completed the time breakdown, he realised to his surprise that he spent over twenty-four hours a week in front of the television set!

You might find that you too have been spending your time doing things that are not important to you. What changes are you going to make to ensure that you're living life, instead of just existing through it?

### *Unwarranted or unnecessary criticism*

When close family or friends criticise us, most of us will ask for details about their concerns. But some of us have people in our lives that take great pleasure in criticising us about every little thing. Personally, we don't care what they think about us or what we do, but we may have to be courteous to them anyway. Should we give them a reward for their nasty comments by getting upset or defensive (which is probably what they want us to do?) Instead of reacting when they criticise us unfairly, we should short-circuit their manipulative games by doing the following:

Calmly acknowledging to the critic that there *may* be some truth in what s/he says. This allows you to receive criticism comfortably, without becoming anxious or defensive and gives no reward to those using the manipulative criticism.

For example:

Agree with the truth:
> *'I don't like the colour of the jacket you're wearing.'*
> *'I guess I could wear another colour.'*

Agree with the possibility - however slightly:
> *'You're not very careful.'*

*'Maybe I'm not very careful.'*

Agree with logic:
> *'If we bought a new truck now instead of keeping the old clunker, we'd be a lot safer on the road and wouldn't have these high repair bills.'*
> *'You're right. A new truck would have those advantages.'*

Rather than:
> *'There you go - another way to spend our money!'*

Allow for Improvement:
> *'Your suits don't fit you correctly.'*
> *'I'm sure they could fit better.'*

Empathy:
> *'You're being very unfair.'*
> *'I can see how you feel that I'm unfair.'*

Because you don't react negatively (which they expected and hoped you'd do) they'll likely stop harassing you and direct their criticism towards another target.

### *Jumping to Conclusions*

Have you ever jumped to a conclusion and ended up with egg on your face because you responded incorrectly? Unfortunately, society often gives stereotypes to people and it's hard for individuals to maintain an unbiased attitude towards others. Do you make comments that identify your biases?

For example: do you make comments that start out with:

> *'All girls are...'*
> *'Men/women are...'*
> *'You know what she's like!'*
> *'I could never tell her that!'*
> *'I was born this way.'*
> *'You'll never change her mind.'*
> *'It's the same everywhere.'*
> *'Nothing will ever change.'*
> *'This always happens!'*
> *'Do I have to spell it out?'*
> *'He would never believe me!'*
> *'Everybody does it...'*

Catch yourself if you find yourself jumping to conclusions or stereotyping others. If others are stereotyping you, identify your findings to them and ask them to identify why they made the assumptions and made the comments they did.

## *Truly Incorrigible Difficult People*

How do you handle people who trigger your defence mechanism when they walk into the room? This type of difficult person isn't just someone who's having a bad day or with whom you're having a personality conflict. Instead, this difficult person is difficult often - and often difficult with everyone. These people have many negative ways of expressing anger. Some are destructive, not only to the angry person, but to those around them. For instance, they:

- Yell at or blame others;
- Give verbal abuse - sarcasm or ridicule;
- Use physical violence;
- Give threats to others;
- Resort to temper tantrums (see chapter 4);
- Use *"the silent treatment"* or withdraw;
- Deny or buck-pass;
- Vandalise property; or abuse drugs or alcohol.

Do you still want to or must associate with this person? If you don't, you may decide to stay away from this person.

When faced with having to deal with a truly incorrigible person, you might find that rehearsing the problem behaviour or situation with another, will get you through it with the least amount of difficulty. Your friend should have as much knowledge of the situation as possible. This way, s/he can formulate good arguments and can anticipate what the other person's objections or reactions might be. The adage that practice makes perfect, works here. Remember that the person you're eventually going to deal with has not had the opportunity to practice.

This is especially valuable when you're having problems with those in a position of power, such as a parent or older person.

# CHAPTER 2

# WHAT KIND OF PERSON ARE YOU?

## *Personality Types*

Before we learn how to deal with difficult people, it's important for you to identify not only your personality style, but also that of your difficult people. We can change how we deal with others, so we'll be more on their *"wave length"* and can match their communication needs. We're all a mixture of these four personality types, but one should match more clearly than the others. To do this:

From the information given below (reading the strengths and descriptions below each type) choose the personality type closest to your behaviour pattern. This will require you to look inside yourself to determine what you feel and do in *"real life"*.

## *YOUR STRENGTHS*

### *Type A: Strengths*

Direct; outgoing; up-front; stimulating; people skilled; persuasive; risk-taker; competitive and self-assured.

These people are spontaneous, often employed in sales and are people-people - they want respect from others. Others may feel they're aggressively competitive in their pursuit of what they want. They dislike people who lack enthusiasm, keep them waiting, are indecisive or rigid or those who go by the book. They love attention, a sense of achievement and crave recognition, adventure and excitement.

### *Type B Strengths:*

Practical; ambitious; efficient; methodical; direct; results-oriented; conventional; resolute; deter-mined; organised and dependable.

These people make good entrepreneurs and directors. They like to direct and take charge of things. They're task-oriented and must always win. They hate emotional people, ambiguity, disrespect and laziness in others. They like others to be controlled, loyal, to keep a fast pace and like responsibility.

## *Type C: Strengths:*

Team-oriented; trusting; warm; faithful; enthusiastic; co-operative; approachable; sensitive; good listener; good friend; likes change; outgoing and ambassador.

These people are often in the service industry (hospitality, health care, transportation, social services) because they have a strong desire to help others. They hold in stress and store it away - seldom putting themselves first. They're protective of the underdog, want everyone to love them and are often passive in their behaviour. They dislike insensitive, argumentative, insincere or egotistical people. They like others who are warm, kind and caring.

## *Type D: Strengths:*

Rigid; meticulous; accurate; inhibited; painstaking; sensible; serene; high standards and avoids risks.

These are more detail-oriented than people-people. They enjoy working alone, often in accounting, technical or engineering fields. They dislike people who are fakes, overly assertive, careless or arrogant. They like those who are perfectionists, consistent, informed, practical, good workers and are easy to get along with.

It's now time to choose which type suits your personality the best before you go on to the next section. After choosing your type, look at the weaknesses of your chosen personality type. These are typical weaknesses for the types of personalities and can make *you* a difficult person to others. You may have eliminated many of these negative traits, but you'll likely recognise many that you'll need to work on.

### YOUR WEAKNESSES

## *Type A: Weaknesses:*

Browbeater; domineering; restless; impatient; pushy; manipulative; grating; reactive and controlling.

## *Type B Weaknesses:*

Uncaring; critical; frugal; unyielding; aloof; uncompromising; distant; insistent; stubborn; inflexible and inaccessible.

## *Type C: Weaknesses:*

Too empathetic; indecisive; unreasonable; defenceless; wishy-washy; subjective; hesitant; irrational; vulnerable; pushover; passive; pleases others and walked-on.

## *Type D: Weaknesses:*

Procrastinates; perfectionist; unsociable; uninteresting; brooding; bashful; passive; hates change and monotonous.

Do everything you can to try to correct the weaknesses you have that make you a difficult person to others.

### *Dealing with your difficult people*

Then analyse the information to determine the personality of your difficult people. This requires a high degree of empathy - you'll have to place yourself in their shoes to come up with an accurate analysis of your difficult people.

List your difficult people giving their name. Then determine their personality type from the earlier information.

## Name and personality type

1._____

2._____

3._____

4._____

### *How to work with other personality types:*

If you're in a working or personal relationship with someone of these types, here are a few things that may be helpful to remember:

## A Type

- Give praise, credit and recognition regularly.
- Be sociable with them.
- Treat them as if what they're doing is important.
- Encourage them to use their creative abilities.
- If they're hyperactive, re-channel their energies - help them choose priorities.

## B Type

- Give them as much control as possible.
- Give loose supervision - lots of rope.
- Make them feel important.
- Utilise their efficient, practical and ambitious nature.
- Use their organisational abilities.
- Respect their conventional values and methods.
- Be flexible in accepting their way of doing things.

## C Type

- Don't get upset with their need to have everyone like them.
- Treat others even more fairly when in their presence.
- Be up-front in your dealings with them.
- Give them opportunities to mingle with others.
- Have patience with their indecisive behaviour.

## D Type

- Listen to their ideas.
- Help them set deadlines.
- Give them room to do the job their way.
- Use logic and facts in discussions.
- Show respect.

Look at *the "Working with Type As, Bs, Cs and Ds"* and see how you could get along better with others. It's often impossible to get others to adapt their personality to match ours, so it's up to us to try to adapt to theirs.

Next determine what adjustments you should take to adapt your communication style to make it more in tune with that of your difficult people. (To do this, you must be willing to adapt your personality style to come closer to theirs. Remember you likely *can't* change their behaviour, but you *can* change your reaction to their behaviour.)

***What could you change in your approach to them that would improve the situation?***

1._____

2_____

3. _____

4. _____

The more we know about the personality type of another, the better we can adapt our behaviour so we're on the same or similar *"wave length"* as others.

## *Work on your weaknesses.*

For instance, if you're an *'A'* type personality - it's possible that you're perceived by others as being too controlling, pushy, domineering; as being impatient (don't give them enough time to make decisions comfortably) and your restlessness can border on hyperactivity. If two *'A'* type personalities work together (or are married to each other) you can bet that both will be fighting for control.

If you're a *'B'* type personality – others may see you as uncaring (even though you <u>are</u> caring). They may see you as being too critical, stubborn and inflexible. You'll need to bend a bit more. If two *'B'* types work together their inflexible and stubborn personalities could cause much strife.

If you're a *'C'* type - you may sit on the fence too long - hate making decisions and the *'A'* types will be after you to decide long before you're ready to make one. Others may take advantage of you and walk all over you because of your too-often empathetic response to others' needs.

If you're a *'D'* type, your habit of perfectionism and procrastination along with your habit of digging in your heels when faced with change, can make you many enemies. Most *'D'* types have problems communicating their ideas to others verbally.

## *Manipulation*

Most people use rational tactics including logic and bargaining to show they're willing to comply or compromise to find the best solution to differences. They negotiate by giving up a little, if the other person agrees to do the same. But many use underhanded methods to get others to do what they want them to do. This is through manipulation that can be towards good or bad ends. Many find both positive and negative manipulation effective for influencing others to do what they want. Positive manipulation is good; because it helps others improve their lives. This manipulation includes giving praise, recognition and encouragement and is welcomed.

*"Game players"* however, use negative manipulation to acquire what they want using passive resistant, indirect aggressive, aggressive or passive/aggressive behaviour. Negative manipulation is destructive, underhanded and sneaky. It's used to get others to do something they don't want to do. These people may use ridicule, anger or shouting to get others to meet their demands or through *"soft soaping"* the other person. Both are effective, but people often retaliate against the manipulator when they find themselves doing something they had no intention of doing.

Many playing games aren't even aware they're doing so and can't understand why others are so upset by their behaviour. Although some may achieve a temporary sense of power - others distrust them if they're caught playing their games.

What tactics do you use when you're trying to persuade someone to do something? Do you use power and control, giving the person the impression that they must *'Do it your way or else...?'* Or do you go out of your way to humble yourself, flattering the person or acting overly nice, *'I know you feel your way is best, but couldn't you do it this way, just this once?'*

Those who use passive resistance normally harm only themselves, because others see right through their manipulation. Some are whiners, complainers and bellyachers, but do nothing to change their situations. Their methods don't always work, because their manipulation is often so subtle, that others may miss their veiled messages.

The more hostile personality will use indirect aggression, which demonstrates hidden antagonism. This is shown by the person's behaviour that shouts out their hostility. Targets of this hostility are often at those in authority. They use sabotage, sarcasm, *"the silent treatment"*, sulking, gossip and backhanded compliments.

Passive-aggressive behaviour not only harms the person in the long run, but others as well. These people are often charming, which makes it all the harder to figure out why they are driving you around the bend. It's not that they make cruel or sarcastic comments or indulge in temper tantrums. On the contrary, they never get mad - they play the injured innocent if you accuse them of being upset - yet they manage to leave you feeling guilty, stupid or frustrated. Some days you may wonder if you're going insane when around these people. You may often feel guilty and as if you were the person in the wrong but can't put a finger on what the passive/aggressive person did that triggered that response.

Passive-aggressives behave as they do because anger (repressed in early childhood) is forced underground and is not allowed to surface. Overbearing or neglectful parents, a reaction to divorce or death, could have caused this reaction and its fear of some kind that forbids them to directly express their hostility.

Passive-aggression is not a mental illness, such as schizophrenia. It's an unconscious personality disorder – a learned behaviour – in which passivity is used to mask hidden aggression. Often those harbouring it, are unaware that it exists. They infuriate their friends and family with lateness, procrastination and calculated inefficiency. It usually takes a therapist to help them recognise their pattern of behaviour and overcome the problems it causes.

If you want to do a more thorough investigation of the forms of manipulation, I suggest you get my book ***Dealing with Difficult People*** that concentrates one full chapter on identifying the 115 ways people try to manipulate others (and how to deal with them).

### *How your behaviour affects others*

It's important when interacting with others that you understand the impact your actions may have on others' emotions and responses.

Here's an example of a situation - let's see what behaviour you would respond with:

You only have one hour to go to the store to pick up groceries and complete several errands. You get to the store to find that the store jammed with shoppers. You finally get close to the end of the check-out line. Someone stops to chat with the person ahead of you and makes moves to ease into the line in front of you. How would you react?

a) Let the person stay, muttering about people who butt into line.
b) Ask the person to go to the back of the line, explaining that you've been waiting a long time.
c) Say nothing.
d) Bawl them out for their rudeness and tell them to go to the back of the line.
e) Make a sarcastic remark about their behaviour.

Which did you choose? The right answer is (b). What kind of behaviour did the person butting in display? Right - they were acting aggressively. Would you have felt that *you* were acting aggressively if you did (b)?

29

You shouldn't, because what you were doing was standing up for your rights – acting assertively.

Here's an explanation of the responses identified:

a)  Passive resistance.
b)  Assertive.
c)  Passive.
d)  Aggressive.
e)  Indirect aggression.

The following will help if you find out whether you allow others to walk all over you (passive) or you've alienated others by using forceful behaviour (aggressive).

## *Behaviour Styles*

There are three basic kinds of behaviour:

### Passive:

These people seldom (if ever) express their own desires and needs. Instead, they give in to the demands, needs and desires of others. They're reluctant to defend their rights and stand up for themselves. Their behaviour shows that they don't respect themselves. For example:

> Mark: *'Where do you want to go for lunch today? Should we go to Roberto's (Italian food) or to The Wok (Chinese food)?'*
> Sheldon: *'I don't care (he likes Chinese food).'*
> Mark: *'I feel like spaghetti - so let's go to Roberto's!'*
> Sheldon: *'Okay, if you want to.'*

Sheldon acted passively and didn't let Mark know where he wanted to go. Sheldon expected Mark to guess what he wanted. This seldom happens, so Mark got his way while Sheldon quietly fumed.

### Aggressive:

These people show little respect for the needs and desires of others - everything must go their way. They lack empathy and have difficulty placing themselves in another's shoes. They take advantage of others, especially if they show weakness or can't defend themselves (for instance, they're rude to a waiter or waitress). Another example:

> Sandy: *'Barry, can you give me a ride home tonight?'*
> Barry: *'I can't. I have to go grocery shopping after work.'*

Sandy: *'That's okay. I have to pick up some groceries too.'*
Barry: *'I'd rather not tonight.'*
Sandy: *'How come?'*
Barry: *'It's just not convenient for me - I'll be rushed as it is.'*
Sandy: *'I'd do it for you! Some friend you are!'*

Sandy had the right to ask Barry for a ride, but when she tried to force her wishes and desires on him, her behaviour became aggressive. She forced Barry to defend himself and tried to make Barry feel guilty when he wouldn't comply with her wishes.

## Assertive:

Their attitude towards others shows that they respect themselves. They're comfortable when they express their needs and defend their rights when necessary. As well, they respect the right of others to express their needs and defend their rights. For example:

Mark: *'Where do you want to go for lunch today? Should we go to Roberto's (Italian food) or to The Wok (Chinese food)?'*
Sheldon: *'I prefer The Wok. How about you?'*
Mark: *'My mouth is watering for some spaghetti.'*
Sheldon: *'I don't mind having that today. Let's go there.'*
Mark: *'Let's make plans to go to The Wok next Tuesday, okay?'*
Sheldon: *'Sure, sounds good to me!'*

Both people win in this exchange. Try to use assertive behaviour most of the time. Nobody can force you to give up your rights. The only person who can give up those rights is you - the person who owns them. You become less of a person, if you give up your rights to another (unless you determine it's best for both parties).

In addition to the three kinds of basic behaviour mentioned earlier, there are three others:

## Passive Resistant:

These are passive people who are trying to become more assertive in their behaviour. They mutter and sigh a lot and play manipulative games to get their way. They haven't learned how to ask directly for what they want. For example:

Joey: *'Mom, can you drive me to school today?'*

His mother had her morning planned. It was a beautiful day and Joey as usual had been fooling around until he was late leaving for school.

Mom: *'Joey, I've driven you twice this week...'*

Joey: *'Oh Mom... please?'*

Mom: (letting out a big sigh) *'Oh, all right!'*

Her body language and speech say, *'Just look at the sacrifices I make for you. If you loved me more, you'd appreciate me more!'*

People should look at their actions realistically. For instance, overweight people often use the excuse that *'Fat runs in my family'* as the cause for their extra pounds when the fact is that nobody *runs* in his or her family. Their exercise normally involves walking to the fridge to get something to eat while they watch television.

**Indirect Aggressive:**

These people are between assertive and obviously aggressive. They use subtle, underhanded ways to get their way, such as sabotage, sarcasm, sulking, the silent treatment and gossip. For example:

Don: *'My wife wants me to clean the basement this weekend. I'm going to give it a stab, but I won't clean it to her standards. Then maybe she won't expect me to do that job again.'* (Sabotage).

Jane: *'I see you finally decided to get your hair cut in a style that suits you.'* (Sarcasm).

Linda hadn't spoken to her husband George for four days following an argument. They hadn't resolved the issue and George had tried several times to get her to talk about the problem - she refused. (Silent treatment).

Linda: *'Ask your father to pass the salt.'* (Sulking)

Jill: *'Did you hear about Carmen's husband? He was picked up for drunk driving last night.'* (Gossip).

**Passive-aggressive:**

These people have a pathological reaction to authority and those they perceive in positions of authority. They channel their aggression into passive behaviour by slowing the efforts of others and stonewalling progress. They're often the bottleneck that holds up completion of tasks. They try to control without confrontation and their actions could involve hidden sabotage. Most are very charming and specialize in aggression that's easy to deny and hard to prove.

Passive-aggressives always seem to anticipate the other person's next step and are there to provide further roadblocks to progress. They love insubordination. Some are great sulkers and will keep at it until they get their way. They can be very hard to detect, and others often feel frustrated when dealing with them, but don't always understand why.

As most of us grow up, we're faced with restrictions that are normal and necessary. People with this tendency have often been controlled excessively, so when they were growing up they learn to control others without confrontation. They love the thrill of insubordination and it sometimes doesn't matter if they win as long as it appears their opponents loose. They love to play win-lose games and put something over on others.

They use excuses such as: *'It's not my fault this didn't work; it's yours.'* They show frequent signs of helplessness. The simplest action seems beyond their comprehension. When others are dealing with them, they provoke feelings of defensiveness. They're either late completing most of their tasks or don't finish them. When prodded, they become argumentative. They're backstabbers, gossipers and are often so good at it that others believe their falsehoods.

Most people display the above signs at one time or another. However, if this develops into being their normal behaviour, these people are likely passive-aggressives. Those who deal with them will have to remain on guard. Confront them using facts when you *"catch them in the act"*. Make sure they understand the consequences of their actions, *'If this happens again, I'll...'*

Some serious passive aggressives have criminal tendencies. These people get a thrill out of speeding, of drinking and driving - and getting away with it. In some, this tendency keeps accelerating, because they require higher and higher levels of danger, thrills and excitement to keep them appeased.

Passive-aggressive behaviour not only harms the person, but others as well. Those who show this tendency have a pathological reaction to authority figures.

## *Traditional Behaviour*

**Men:** Traditional men believe that their role in life is to be strong, decision-makers, competitive and aggressive. To adapt to the new thinking in society, men are being forced to change. They're acting less aggressively, are more empathetic and in tune with their feelings and the feelings of others although many of them would still fail if given emotional intelligence testing.

Imagine men blushing like brides, crying like babies and giggling like schoolgirls. New evidence suggests nature intended men to be at least as emotionally expressive as women. Traditionally, young male children are taught to shut down and wall-off their emotions. This has left many men in a masculinity crisis - unprepared for the demands of modern manhood and vulnerable to such things as stress-related illness or alcoholism. Big boys are simply not supposed to cry!

In fact, boys start out more emotionally expressive than girls. One study showed that even at six months of age, boys demonstrated significantly more joy and anger were more vocal, fussy and cried more than girls. Society converted these emotionally gifted baby boys into emotionally stunted men. Mothers worked harder to manage their more excitable and emotional male babies and kept them quiet. Unwittingly, they taught baby boys to turn down their emotional volume. Dad was at work, so boys talked almost exclusively to their mothers about their feelings and talked to their dads about sports. Dad provided the house to live in, while Mom made it a home. It was important to fathers that their sons are masculine, and their peer group completed the job. When boys played together, it was usually in structured games where things like toughness, teamwork and stoicism were valued and learned. By six years of age it was clear that these boys had emotionally shut down.

This shutting down was successful in an earlier era where harsh social conditions of backbreaking work and world wars required a tough, armour-like kind of masculinity. So, boys were raised to be just like their fathers or grandfathers. However, back then roles were more clear-cut. Women raised the children and men were the breadwinners. This style of socialization doesn't fit today's era very well. Now, men share the breadwinning and child-care roles with their wives - but many men still don't feel right in the part. They are still ill equipped emotionally to do it, because they're unable to tune into their own feelings and therefore have difficulty doing so with their wives and children.

If someone pushed a boy down on the playground, he was supposed to come back with a fistful of dirt - not a face full of tears. So, when hurt, ashamed or even afraid - men were taught to react aggressively. This is clearly dysfunctional in a family relationship. Men grow up ashamed of showing affection and in adulthood they express affection almost solely through sex.

Thankfully - what has been learned - can be unlearned. The emotional skills required these days can lead to a satisfying life as empathetic husband, father and individual in society. Men who have done this, have found their lives better because they're able to assume the role of nurturing fathers and companions to their wives. Many of their fathers envy the closeness they observe between their sons, their wives and their children and wonder why they don't have the same closeness with their wives and children. This only happens if the men are willing to change. For many, it's simply too much trouble.

**Women:** Many women also continue to follow the traditional behaviour of their mothers and grandmothers. They believe that passive behaviour is normal and accepted behaviour for women. Therefore, they believe that women who compete or become too powerful are un-feminine and aggressive. Some, in their attempts to change however, have gone to the other extreme and have become aggressive themselves. Most women who succeed in business have found the happy medium.

### *Worry*

Are you a worrywart - constantly worried about your family, your finances, your job, your health and the weather? Do you worry about unimportant things such as a spot on your slacks, dust under the TV or that you forgot an important occasion?

Constant worrying can cause or aggravate all kinds of health problems including migraines, sore neck and back, ulcers and heart problems. So how should constant worriers deal with life? Start by taking control of those worries. Put them into two groups - those you can do something about - and those you can't. Then tackle the first group and ignore the second. As soon as you catch yourself worrying, distract yourself by calling a friend, looking out the window, going for a drive - anything to distract you.

Here are some other steps you can take to help yourself with worry:

1.  Analyze your worries. Most people worry - but some overdo it. Worry tends to motivate most to take the necessary action. Others react by avoiding the situation by *not* acting. Worrying offers an illusion of control. Some believe if they worry enough - magically it will prevent the bad thing from happening! It's a form of burying their heads in the sand. These people are truly out of control of their lives. They wait for something to happen, but seldom *make* things happen. They need to get cracking and do something about their worries, instead of just letting them fester and contaminate everything positive they try to do.

2.  Don't let yourself get caught up in a catch-22 situation. Once negative thinking takes hold, the person's negative thoughts can quickly get out of hand. The mind is very imaginative and will think up all kinds of weird and frightening things that could possibly happen.

3.  Recognise that the worry you're suffering can cause serious hazards to your health. The stress involved is probably playing havoc with you physically, emotionally and mentally. Know that it's important for you to keep your stress to tolerable levels. Between fifty and eighty per cent of the reasons people visit their doctor are attributed to stress and excessive anxiety. The key lies in recognizing the worry for what it is and letting the thought slip away without giving attention to it. This is not always easy to do. Lighten up! Worrying is bad for your health (as if you didn't have enough to worry about).

4.  You're not alone if you're a worrier. In a recent survey, more than half the people polled said they worry so much, that worry itself is a significant problem. Women worry more than men and college students more than senior citizens.

5.  Worry can cause physiological harm and can shorten a person's life. Worriers not only die younger, but also have different attributes from those who don't chronically worry.

6.  Spend some time daily mulling over problems you're facing. Give yourself only a set time to worry, but be willing to spend more, if you're on a problem-solving roll. During that time, solve as many of the problems you're worrying about as possible. This way, you'll confine worry to a specific time, that will allow you to turn off your worries after you've dealt with them.

7.  Try scheduling a worry time into your day. Many therapists suggest that people schedule a 30-minute worry time into their day - but never within an hour of bedtime. That way, when worry at

other times threatens to distract them from the job they're doing, they can remind themselves there's time later in the day to deal with the problem. When the worry time arrives, if they've forgotten some of what they intended to think over, it wasn't very important. If daytime worry is a problem, focused-breathing exercises are often helpful. If insomnia is a problem - relaxation exercises can work as a sedative.

8.    Recognise when you're beginning to worry. Worrying tends to sneak up on people, so it's important to be sensitive to our thought patterns. Tell yourself that you'll spend adequate time dealing with it at your *"worry time"*. Then, remove it from your mind.

If you find you're still worrying - use negative reinforcement. Place an elastic band loosely around your wrist and snap it hard every time you catch yourself dwelling on those things you've decided you can't do anything about.

Chronic worriers can spot negative aspects and even potential danger in almost any situation. People prone to worry will magnify the danger involved. Although worry is a potentially harmful pastime, people continue worrying, because they derive some sense of benefit from it.

Kim could handle her worries about work and financial matters, but her life turned into a tailspin when her cat died. She found that she couldn't sleep. The harder she tried the less sleep she got. After seeing several doctors, including a psychiatrist and neurologist, she finally found help at a sleep disorder clinic. Psychologists say that stress often takes its toll on the body in the form of insomnia.

At bedtime, people lie quietly, without distraction from their day's activities. However, that's also when they have time to think about the cares, woes, problems and stressors they've faced during their day.

Why worry about it? Worrying is a useless activity. It takes up your energy and time; time that you could spend solving your problems rather than just worrying about them. Some mental health professionals call worry, an *"anticipatory anxiety"* - because worriers occupy their time expecting future problems. They're likely more self-conscious, daydream more and interpret events differently.

Worrying can be a substitute for acting. Others use worry to avoid scolding or punishment. Children who have done something wrong may state, *'I'm worried.'* Instead of punishing the wrongdoing, the parent may comfort the child to soothe the child's anxiety.

Similarly, if a woman spent too much money shopping, she may go to her husband and say: *'I'm worried about our finances.'* This deflects criticism about the shopping spree. Some use worry, to get attention or to control the behaviour of others.

Some people worry because they're superstitious and see magic in worrying. Some believe that if they worry about something, it won't happen. Others may worry because if the event does happen, they can say, *'See? I told you that would happen!'*

### So, how can you overcome worry?

1. Accept that what you worry about is a problem.
2. Eliminate whatever is causing you to continue worrying.
3. Accept responsibility for dealing with the problem.
4. Deal with the problem.

If you see another person or situation as the cause of the problem - it controls you and can make you feel helpless. By realizing you have control over the problem and can deal with it, the helpless feeling disappears. This enables you to act.

What do you do if the problem is serious?

   a) Imagine the worst-case scenario and come up with the worst that could happen.
   b) Reconcile yourself emotionally to the worst outcome and accept it.
   c) Spend the rest of your time concentrating on taking steps to prevent this outcome.

Worriers need to end the *"all or nothing"* thinking that plagues them. They think that if a solution hasn't worked 100 per cent perfectly - then it hasn't worked at all. We can chip some worries away a little at a time. Setting a goal of reducing worry by ten per cent a week will give a person significantly less stress.

Try the *'So what?'* technique. This involves imagining a problem and then saying, *'So what? If that happens I can...'* and think of a solution.
Another coping technique is to build vigor into your personality. Recognise your ability to influence events in your life. Vigor also teaches individuals to read physical signs of stress and develop

strategies to overcome them. Finally, vigor training suggests that when individuals face stressful situations (over which they have no control) they can bolster their self-confidence by meeting new challenges. The new challenge could be taking up a new sport, for instance.

At bedtime when I find myself worrying, I write down all the information about the problem and try to commit that information to memory. Then I distract myself by reading a book and leave my sub-conscious mind to work on the problem during my sleep. Voila – in the morning I often have a very suitable solution to the problem. I have faith in my subconscious so I'm able to turn off the worry and get a good night's sleep.

### Lethargic, Apathetic and Unhappy?

Do you find that you're feeling lethargic, apathetic and unhappy? It's possible that you're suffering from the *"Winter Blues"*. One of the cures may be to increase the level of stress in your life. This means that you don't sit in front of the television set all weekend or stare out the window mulling over the week's problems. Weekends should be exciting and full, so you can go back to your work Monday, with your batteries recharged. Change the stress and do something different from what you normally do all week. Stop worrying about situations you can't change and do something constructive about those that you can. Pamper yourself; take mini-holidays. Do something special just for yourself (without feeling guilty).

# CHAPTER 3

# COMMUNICATION SKILLS FOR DEALING WITH DIFFICULT PEOPLE

If you find there are too many situations where either you misunderstand others, or they misinterpret your messages, you need to work on your communication skills.

## *Same words - different meanings*

Often words mean different things to different people or even between men and women. I was with a group of people socially when a young woman was discussing a job interview she'd had that morning. Her boyfriend asked her whether she'd accept the job if the company offered it to her.

> *'Well, it would be a real challenge.'* she said
> *'Then, I guess you'd turn it down.'*
> *'Oh no, I'd take it if they offer it to me!'*
> *'But why would you - when it'll be such a difficult position?'*
> *'I'd jump at the chance to get this position. As I explained, this job will be a real challenge for me!'*

The conversation progressed until they ended up in a heated argument. The rest of us sat by, wondering what they were arguing about. It suddenly became apparent that they had entirely different definitions of the word *"challenge"*. We asked them to explain what the word meant to each of them.

The women explained that the word challenge meant that: The position would allow her to grow and stretch - to reach her full potential and would give her a chance to prove herself.

Her male companion believed the word *"challenge"* meant: That someone or something was standing in his way - keeping him from getting what he wanted and that he'd have a fight on his hands and would have to defend himself.

If they had used paraphrasing, they would have eliminated this difficulty.

### Skill of Paraphrasing

This skill deals with the use of words. Paraphrasing means:

* To express meaning in other words.
* A restatement of text or work.
* Giving the meaning another form.
* Amplifying a message.

Paraphrasing is used for simple comments such as, repeating telephone numbers when taking a message. But, how often do you transpose two numbers when taking down the seven or eight simple digits of a phone number? The use of paraphrasing is essential at any time when two people are conversing. Unfortunately, when information isn't clear, people often make assumptions. They don't confirm with the other person that what they *thought* they said was what they meant by their comments.

When using paraphrasing, we often start sentences with:

*'Do you mean that...?'*
*'I want to make sure I understood (was clear about) what you said.'*
*'You say you felt upset when I...'*
*'You want me to...'*

When asking others to paraphrase something back to you, be careful how you ask. For instance, if you say:

*'Do you understand?'* (This doesn't confirm that they **did** understand the information you gave them.)
*'Repeat what I told you to do.'* (This will just get the other person's back up).
*'Did you catch that?'* (A put-down because you're insinuating the receiver wasn't bright enough to pick up the information).

If they misunderstand you, it's much better to make the problem yours.

*'To ensure that I was clear with my instructions, could you tell me the steps you're going to take?'*

### Skill of Feedback

Use feedback in both positive and negative situations. Give positive feedback through recognition and compliments by letting others know when you like something they've said or done. These comments make people feel good about themselves and are very welcome.

Unfortunately, most of us ignore the good things people do or say and concentrate only on the bad. Because this book is about dealing with difficult people, we'll be concentrating on using it under negative or difficult situations, but don't forget the importance of positive feedback.

In feedback, you share your reactions to another person's behaviour, with that person. You discuss how you feel when others act or behave in a certain way. People can't try to change their behaviour unless you let them know that their actions are offensive to you. Letting negative situations build up, only escalates the difficulties between people. Resolve minor difficulties when they occur - don't just collect them for future blowups.

### Process of Feedback

Use negative feedback if something someone has done has upset or irritated you. Identify what they've done that bothers you and give them the opportunity of doing something about it. You're not being fair to others if you don't communicate this to them.

The three steps in the process of feedback are as follows:

a) Describe the problem or situation to the person causing the difficulty.
b) Define what feelings or reactions (anger, sadness, anxiety, hurt or distress) the problem behaviour causes you.
c) Suggest a solution or ask the person to provide a solution.

Here's a sample situation:

One of the men in your family left the toilet seat up *again* and you had another middle-of-the-night splash in the bowl. You've had it with the men in your family and decide to try and change their unacceptable behaviour.

a) Describe the problem or situation to the person causing the difficulty:
   *'Last night one of you left the toilet seat up and I had another bath in the toilet in the middle of the night.'*
b) Define what feelings or reactions:
   *'I was furious, wet, had to change my nightgown and it took me over an hour to get back to sleep.'*
c) Suggest a solution or ask them to provide a solution.
   *'I want both of you to promise that you won't do that again!'*

If you don't practice effective feedback, the following often results:

- Every time the person does anything that bothers you, a small blip occurs on your *"screen of annoyance"*. If you don't deal with the problem or situation and the person repeats his/her behaviour, this leads to;
- Another, bigger blip occurring on your *"screen of annoyance"*. This does *not* have to be for the same reason as the original blip.
- Soon these blips collect, and you have a major blow-up with the person.

Even the most trivial incident can trigger this response. It would be much better it if you handled each blip immediately instead of recording it on your *"screen of annoyance"*. Feedback should be used to let others know when you:

- Don't understand something they've said;
- Disagree with them;
- Think they've changed the subject or are going around in circles;
- Are getting irritated; or
- Feel hurt or embarrassed.

### Feedback Steps

Most people will change undesired behaviour if it's brought to their attention in a kind, non-threatening way. But there are exceptions to the rule. Some just don't care what you think, they feel it's not worth changing to suit you - or they have a habit that's hard to change. Others change their behaviour for a while but slip back to doing it their old way. In situations like this, further feedback steps are necessary.

1. Follow a), b) and c) steps from the Process of Feedback.
2. If they do it again - repeat #1.
3. If they do it a third time:
   (i) Ask the person to explain why s/he's still doing something that s/he knows annoys you.
   (ii) Explain the consequences should the behaviour or situation happens again.
4. Follow through with the consequences.

If your father and/or brother changed their behaviour for a while, but slowly but surely, they forgot - and the toilet bowl incident happened again. This is when both mother and daughter would take more drastic actions to stop the behaviour:

1. Follow a), b) and c) steps from the Process of Feedback.
2. Repeat #1.
3. (i) Ask the person to explain why s/he's still doing something that s/he knows annoys you.
   (ii) Explain the consequences should the behaviour or situation happen again.
4. *'Mom and I will have exclusive use of one bathroom and you fellows will have to use the other and be responsible for the upkeep of that bathroom.'*
5. Follow through with the consequences.

### *Skill of listening*

Another skill people take for granted, is listening. Attentive listening is a process that begins with the listener giving the speaker his or her undivided attention. This builds rapport and shows the speaker that the listener values what they're saying. If a speaker feels rushed (either by verbal or non-verbal hints) or if listeners appear too judgmental, they'll probably clam up.

Here are some facts concerning listening:

- We listen in spurts. Most of us are unable to give hard, close attention to what others say for more than sixty seconds at a time. We concentrate - we let up - then we concentrate again.
- We spend up to 80 per cent of our conscious hours using four basic communication skills; writing, reading, speaking and listening.
- Listening accounts for over fifty percent of that time, so we spend forty percent of our waking time just listening!

Have you ever received specific training on how to listen? Probably not. As a student you probably heard, *'Patti will you stop talking...'* not *'Patti will you please listen.'* and give her the skills so she could do so.

How fast do you think the average person speaks in words per minute? (Keep in mind that personal assistants usually take shorthand at 80-120 w.p.m. and court stenographers at 220 w.p.m.)

Normal speaking speed is 125 - 150 w.p.m. My speaking speed is at least 160 w.p.m. especially when I'm conducting seminars.

What do you think your thinking capability is in w.p.m.? I've heard guesstimates from 50 - 300 w.p.m. The average person can think at the phenomenal speed of 750 - 1,200 w.p.m.!

Then why don't we hear what people tell us? Because our minds are bored - that's why. There's not enough happening to keep our brains occupied when people speak at normal speeds. Even my speed of 160 w.p.m. can't always keep participants motivated. So, what happens? My audience goes on side-trips (tune-outs) where they may be:

- Thinking of examples of something I'm discussing;
- Wondering why their spouse was in such a bad mood that morning;
- Admiring an article of clothing and wonder where the person bought it;
- Thinking it must be time for a coffee break, because they're thirsty;
- Making up a mental list of what they must do when they get back to work.

### Kinds of Bad Listeners:

There are several problem listeners we all need to deal with. Here are a few - see if *you* have one of these frailties:

### Bashful:

Because shy people *expect* others to draw them out, they place emotional demands on everyone they're with. If they don't receive this attention, they *"tune out"*. Most shy people aren't aware of this negative behaviour, nor the demands they place on others. They hoard information and selfishly don't share their good ideas with others.

### Anxious:

Because they lack confidence, they use nervous chatter to fill the void. This mental bluster leaves little room for listening to others and others tune out.

### Argumentative:

They'd argue with Einstein about his theory of relativity! They nitpick small details and break the conversational flow.

46

## Opinionated:

They spend their energy formulating arguments, rather than listening to others' opinions. They often interrupt or begin every other sentence with the word *'But...'* or question others' views. They're usually over-anxious in their attempts to impress others. This usually results in the opposite happening; people tune them out.

## Closed-minded:

These are the most infuriating of bad listeners. They have rigid sets of values; find security in their prejudices. Any new ideas or changes leave them feeling threatened and they seldom give in to others' views.

When faced with these poor listeners, use feedback to explain how you feel. Using tact and empathy will allow you to help them be better listeners. Explain to the closed-minded person that they've shut you out - appear unwilling to even listen to your ideas. Tell them that their actions make you feel rejected and unimportant. Once you've explained this to the person and they still behave the same way, you have two choices:

- Put up with their rudeness or
- Use steps 2 to 4 of Feedback Steps

Most closed-minded people don't realise the rut they've fallen into. Your feedback comments might be helpful in changing their attitude and behaviour.

### *Blocks to Effective Listening:*

There are other distractions that can lead us astray when we're listening. Which of the following situations cause problems for you?

1. You had trouble understanding the speaker's words. (They used uncommon language or jargon).
2. While the speaker was talking, you were thinking of what you were going to say.
3. You know you have prejudices, but s/he really tested them.
4. You listened for what *you* wanted to hear.
5. You didn't have enough knowledge to grasp the message. (Their language was too technical, or they used *"big"* words to impress others).
6. You were too tired mentally to work at paying attention.
7. There were outside noises and distractions.

8. The speaker had poor delivery - slow, windy, irrelevant, rambling or repetitious.
9. Something the speaker said intrigued you; you thought about it and when you *"tuned back in"* you'd lost the thread of the conversation.
10. The speaker had an accent and you had difficulty understanding him/her. (This takes considerable concentration and listeners often tune out because they're too tired mentally, to continue the interpretation process).
11. You were too far ahead of the speaker by trying to make them understand ideas too soon.
12. You forgot to use paraphrasing and feedback to ensure you were listening effectively.
13. You felt the speaker was giving you far too much information.

### *Non-verbal Communication*

What are you telling others by your non-verbal communication? Non-verbal communication, body language and the scientific study of kinesics all read a person's unconscious body movements and sounds. We learn how to hide our true feelings, but rarely, if ever, do we turn in a perfect performance. We all use another, deeper level of communication, one that carries the message of who we really are and what we really mean. This is the subconscious, a part of us we have not been able to teach to hide our true feelings. And it leaks out all the time into our surface behaviour, into what we say - the way we say it - and the way our bodies react. These signs include:

- Tone of voice;
- Facial expression;
- Posture;
- Eye contact;
- Touching;
- Gestures;
- Spatial distance; and
- Clothing.

Being able to read others' non-verbal communication is probably one of the best assets anyone can have. We read others, more by what they're showing with their non-verbal communication or body language, than by anything they might say verbally. Examples of how we read body language.

48

You know someone is angry because they have:

- A red face;
- Clenched jaw;
- Loud voice;
- Stamped their foot or pounded the table;
- Flashing eyes;
- Rigid posture;
- Hands on hips or across chest.

You know when someone is embarrassed because they have:

- A red face;
- Tears or cry;
- Quivering voice;
- Dejected body posture;
- Sheepish looks.

### Space Bubbles

We all have a *"space bubble"* of safety around us. For many people, this bubble extends about 18 - 24 inches away from their bodies. Filling their personal space by gesturing makes them appear confident. On the other hand, folding their arms, slouching and making themselves small - signals timidity.

Not only do we have *"space bubbles"* around us, but ownership extends to anything we think belongs to us. This may be our bedroom, kitchen or workshop, our car or boat or our brush and comb. Others may use these articles, but only when we've given them permission to do so. Therefore, we react so violently when someone takes something that belongs to us without asking permission.

People have a psychological upper hand when they're in their own *"territory"*. Therefore, people are most comfortable in their own surroundings - on their own *"turf"*. The next most comfortable space is somewhere neutral (such as a restaurant, a beach or a place that doesn't *"belong"* to either person). The least comfortable place (as far as comfort is concerned) is normally on the other person's *"turf"*. Keep this in mind should you expect a confrontation with another person. If possible, have the confrontation on your *"turf"*.

49

## *Eye Contact*

Eye contact is more than just eye contact. It's more like face contact. You watch the person's expressions, read lips, etc. to pick up what they're saying. Comfortable eye-to-eye contact is a short three seconds - then the person looks away. If you hold direct eye contact longer than three seconds, you'll invade the person's body space, as easily as if you've touched them.

Many aggressive people use this to intimidate others. They could be fifty feet away from the other person, but the person will still feel this invasion of his/her space. When they're mad, they'll likely keep eye contact longer than that - with a mad look on their face. This can be very intimidating to the receiver and is a use of power.

## *Lying*

When people are proud of what they've accomplished, they're open with their body language and they show their hands openly. When they feel guilty or suspicious, they hide their hands either in their pockets or behind their backs. If you accuse them of something, they'll likely give you an incredulous look and reply, *'Who me?'* To try to make you believe them more, they'll usually put their hand on their chest (a non-verbal sign of honesty). The hand to the chest gesture when used by women is often a protective gesture showing sudden surprise or shock.

Additional body language identifies whether the person is lying with several of the following signs:

- They'll not look at you (look down usually);
- Blink their eyes rapidly;
- Twitch and swallow repeatedly;
- Clear their throat and wet lips;
- Hand covers mouth when speaking;
- Shrug their shoulders;
- Rub their nose;
- Scratch their head while talking;
- Put their hand on throat; and/or
- Rub the back of their neck.

The last gesture is the most obvious sign of lying in men and will happen either while he is lying or within sixty seconds of lying. But it also can mean that he's exasperated with the situation - so don't jump to conclusions.

There are crucial differences in the lies women and men tell. When women lie, they tend to focus on making others feel better – such as the woman who tells a friend that her outfit is *"lovely"* even as she cringes looking at it. At the heart of many men's lies, however, is the male ego. Men lie to build themselves up or to conceal something and are more likely to lie to enhance themselves than women are. Consistent lying – even about minor matters – can unglue a marriage or partnership. Men have a hard time admitting failure. How our culture defines success is important to a man, so he assumes that it's important to his partner as well.

Usually as trust builds between men and women, the man stops using such lies. However, a man who can't be honest about his failures in life may end up blaming his wife when things get tough in their marriage. One of the most lied-about subjects is sex. Kind lies can be too much of a good thing if a man habitually says only what his partner wants to hear. It sets the woman up for rude awakenings. If he's complimented her on a dress she's wearing, and it simply doesn't suit her, he's not doing her any favour by complimenting her on it.

One couple, both executives, was worried about losing their jobs, but neither wanted to worry the other and their secrecy exacted a heavy price. Because they both were secretly looking for work elsewhere and were unexpectedly late coming home - both began wondering if the other was cheating on them. Thankfully, both came clean and they were able to assist each other in finding a suitable position.

Occasionally there is a lot to lose by telling the truth and something to be gained by not telling the truth, but it's important to remember that lies are deceptions and repeated deceptions can destroy relationships. A partner who is hearing too many lies needs to have a serious discussion with the partner. Telling the truth to a spouse is the first step in showing that love is more important than lies and builds trust between them.

### How you appear to others

How long do you take to size up others? Five, ten minutes or even less? Surveys show that others decide in the first four minutes whether they like you or not. Your appearance is extremely important to your feelings of self-confidence as well as your impressions on others. If you look good - you usually feel good. Good grooming is a must. This doesn't only mean dressing well, but cleanliness both in your dress and personal grooming.

Many people create a negative impression on others. See if you need to improve any of the following:

a) Too much or too little perfume, after-shave or cologne?
b) Improper hairstyle or cut?
c) Body odour from lack of bathing or wearing clothing for more than one day?
d) Men who are not clean-shaven, moustache or beard scruffy?
e) Women not making the most of themselves with makeup, either too much or too little?
f) Wearing badly outdated or unsuitable style of clothing?
g) Un-coordinated outfits or poor colour sense of what does or does not go together?
h) Dirty, spotted, torn or wrinkled clothing?

Some wear colours that don't suit them. For instance, one man had been working as a project engineer and normally worked on-site, so naturally wore construction clothing. He was having physical problems from working in adverse weather conditions and searched to find an indoor position of some sort. His problems occurred when it was time to change his image. He admitted that he didn't have many suits so would have to buy a new wardrobe. His problem was that he didn't know what colours or styles to buy.

He normally wore earth tone colours but changed his wardrobe after he was colour draped. Instead of wearing earth tone colours, he wore a blue-grey suit (with complementary shirt, tie, socks and shoes) that set off his grey hair to perfection. The image he gave was of a distinguished, mature man (which was the image he wished to portray). Not only did he look better in the colours that suited him, but he felt better too. Now before he buys anything to add to his wardrobe, he checks his colour chart. This way, no matter what he takes out of the closet, the colour will suit him.

If you haven't been colour draped to find the colours that suit you best, you're probably wasting hundreds of dollars a year. Look in your closet and see how many items you've bought that are still sitting on their hangers, because they *"just don't feel right"*.

### Interrupters

When good friends converse with each other (especially women) they often interrupt each other and finish each other's sentences. This is unacceptable in a business setting or if the people are virtual strangers to each other. If others have interrupted you in a rude way and you find you're getting a bit *"miffed"*, address the person who has interrupted you. Put out your hand and say in a polite but firm voice, *'Excuse me, Melodye, I'm not finished.'* Then continue with what you were going to say. Don't make eye contact with her because this invites further interruptions.

After you've spoken, direct the conversation back to the person who interrupted you by making eye contact, extending your hand and saying, *'Thanks Melodye. You were saying?'*

If you wish to be an interrupter yourself, the least offensive way to interrupt is to acknowledge that you're doing it. Put your hand in a stopping motion and say, *'Melodye, before you go on, I'd like to make a point.'*

### Stuck Record Technique

In this age of telemarketing, we've all answered the telephone to hear someone explaining her company's rug cleaning special. We all know when the caller identifies herself and asks how your day is going - that a sales pitch will follow. Here's how you can deal with persistent sales types:

> They say, *'We have a rug cleaning special on today.'*
> You, *'I'm not interested in rug cleaning.'*
> They, *'But this special is just good for this week...'*
> You, *'I'm not interested.'*
> They, *'How about having your living room suite cleaned?'*
> You, *'I'm not interested... goodbye.'* And hang up.

Many might feel that this person is just trying to make a living. My answer to this is that they're invading my privacy - if I want rug cleaning, I'll call *them*.

Use the *"stuck-record technique"* in similar situations. This is where you say the same words repeatedly until the person hears what you're saying. Don't raise your voice or get defensive. By the third time you refuse, they usually hear what you're saying. It allows you to remain calm, while ignoring the manipulative ploys they're using against you.

You can use this skill in other situations too. For instance, when someone is trying to convince you to do something you really don't want to do.

Your cousin Peter says, *'Harry, can you drive me home from work tonight?'*
You say, *'No I can't. Sorry I'm busy.'*
Peter, *'Harry, I really need you to drive me home from work tonight. How come you can't drive me?'*
You, *'As I said, I'm too busy.'*

When anyone asks you to explain why you've said no, they're acting aggressively and are trying to take advantage of you. You're under no obligation to tell a person why you can't do what they want you to do. Use this skill whenever you want to say *'No'* to somebody who's trying to convince you to say *'Yes.'* No guilty feelings allowed!

### Teasing

Most teasing is sheer playfulness, but occasionally there's an underlying message to it. When someone is doing something wrong, teasing is a light-hearted way to bring a person's attention to it without making him/her feel bad. That's one of the primary uses of teasing. As a form of indirect communication, teasing performs other functions as well. Teasers may be expressing anger or affection. They may be puffing up wounded self-esteem or doing nothing more than playing.

For many adults uncomfortable with the aspects of intimacy, teasing is a great way to bypass their unease. Some have loving or affectionate feelings towards each other, but the intensity of that affection is difficult for them to manage. They might make a loving statement – then joke about it to diminish the intensity of the moment.

Another example is male repartee. Often, it's obvious that two men teasing each other are very fond of each other.

At one time or another, most of us have teased someone who has irritated us. One way to express anger indirectly - without being pinned down as being hostile - is to do it in a teasing way. Thus, the spouse, relative or in-law who relentlessly heckles you - then says, *'I was just kidding!'* may be quite ticked off with you.

Teasing can be used as a way of repairing a wounded ego, but it can also become a form of bullying. Let's say the youngest, smallest, most frail child at the bus stop is the object of nasty taunts. His ego is likely going to suffer. Yet - if a new child arrives at the bus stop (who's even younger, smaller and frailer) our previous victim won't necessarily show empathy or compassion. He's more likely to turn right around and join in the teasing of this newcomer. This isn't fair - but it's a regular occurrence. Why does it happen? Because the role models in the child's life use it - monkey see - monkey do.

And adults are even crueller with their barbs. Teasing/bullying is a way of life in the sports arena. The coach uses it all the time with his players and at work supervisors bully their staff.

# CHAPTER 4

# DIFFICULT SIBLINGS

## Sibling Rivalry

Sibling rivalry is normal. It's a training ground for children to learn how to get along with others. Parents set the guidelines and step in if activities get out of hand. Children learn how to share toys and people, how to deal with jealousy and how to express joy and anger in safe ways. Parents that have problems with their children should buy an excellent book called, ***P.E.T. - Parent Effective-ness Training,*** by Dr. Thomas Gordon. It's one of the best tools available to help people learn the subtle art of negotiation whether they be adults, teens or children.

As children grow and mature, parents learn to *"bite their tongues"* and refrain from interfering unless their children ask or need them to help. If violence occurs, they then step in. However, life is not always as we would like it to be. The following describes problems that occur in siblings as they mature.

## Personality Differences

*'My sister and I have had to share our bedroom for two years and have an ongoing problem. We're the typical "odd couple". She's very neat and tidy and I'm more comfortable with a lived-in look. Is there any hope for us?'*

It all depends on your individual flexibility. If you're truly flexible, do the following:

1. Each of you writes down complaints about what the other does that bothers you.
2. Determine which complaints you can change or where you can both compromise.
3. Decide whether the compromise would be suitable to each of you.
4. As a last resort, include your parents in the problem-solving process.

## Friends who smoke

*'My brother and I moved away from home into an apartment. He and I don't smoke, but his friends do. I don't want his friends to smoke in our*

*apartment. How can I deal with this without alienating our relationship?'*

Let your brother know how offensive you find this situation. Then try to negotiate a settlement that's satisfactory to both of you. You might compromise when his friends visit the apartment by asking that they use your brother's bedroom as their meeting place. Have the window open in that room or have an ecologizer going or insist they smoke outside the apartment.

Be open to your brother's suggestions as well. It would have been wiser if you had discussed this matter *before* you moved into the apartment together.

### *Procrastinator*

*'My sister and I have the same weekend task. Our home has two bathrooms and we each need to clean one every weekend. We both hate cleaning bathrooms but have different approaches about when we clean them. I get all the unpleasant tasks out of the way at the beginning of my day and finish my tasks with a sense of accomplishment. My sister puts unpleasant tasks off as long as possible, getting more agitated as the day wears on. She ends up snapping at me because the disagreeable tasks are still waiting for her to do. I'm tired of her nasty behaviour.'*

We all have tasks we hate. That doesn't mean we can allow ourselves to do a careless job. Instead, we should get these kinds of jobs out of the way first, so we can enjoy the rest of our day. You're right. Do the distasteful tasks first and encourage your sister to try this technique. If she continues to snap at you, use feedback to explain how that makes you feel.

There are all kinds of procrastinators. Some who procrastinate say *'I'll do it tomorrow'* (which may or may not happen). Sometimes they have too much to do and need to learn how to say *'No'* when necessary. Other procrastinators put off tasks until they're *'Good and ready to do it.'* This gives them a sense of power over the situation.

How can people tell when procrastination is really a problem?

- When they have something important to do, not much time to do it in, but find themselves looking for other activities to do instead.
- When *they* set deadlines, and don't meet them!
- When they constantly delay making important decisions.

- When they work furiously at the last minute to complete crucial assignments.

There are two basic kinds of people who procrastinate more than average:

## The 'Hurry-up' Type

They wait until the last minute and work around the clock to meet deadlines. To correct this behaviour, they need to set concrete deadlines of when they must have tasks completed, remembering to leave some leeway in case they run into problems.

## The 'I'll Decide Tomorrow' Type

They postpone decisions until events resolve the situation or others force a decision upon them. These are normally passive people who are *"fence-sitters"*. They haven't learned that the only thing they'll get from fence sitting - is slivers!

### *Forgetful*

*'My brother is always forgetting to do things he's said he will do. He counts on others to remind him. I'm getting tired of his actions. His usual comments are, 'I thought you were looking after that!' Or, 'I didn't know you wanted me to stop at the store for you.' Or, 'Why didn't you remind me that it was Mom's birthday?'*

These people expect others to look after them, to remind them of things they should do, deadlines that must be met - and who's responsible for what. Don't let him get away with this behaviour. Tell him that from now on - he's on his own - that you're through reminding him to do things. If he forgets - it's all on his shoulders - not yours. Refuse to take any guilt from him when he runs into difficulties and restrain yourself from bailing him out, so he realises you mean what you say.

### *Common-Law Marriage*

*'My twenty-year-old sister has asked my advice. She wants to know if she should move in with her boyfriend. They're contemplating marriage in a few years, but she doesn't know whether she should take the plunge or not. What should I advise her?'*

Give your sister the following information and let her make up her own mind.

Thirty to fifty percent of those under the age of thirty will cohabit before they marry. They're doing it to see if they want to turn the relationship into marriage. They expect that living together will prepare them for it. Many women view living together as a chance to isolate any problems. But living together doesn't always pave the way for marital bliss. The rate of divorce of those who live together is half again as high as it is among those who don't! There are no definite reasons for this, but it's possible that because there's no binding connection in living together, they haven't tried things out. So, when the couple marry, they've never lived together as a married couple and faced all the trials and tribulations that marriage brings.

Simply living together doesn't guarantee they've blended. What's his is his and what's hers is hers. The two may have separate bank accounts and continue spending money on what's important to them as individuals. They may not have done any negotiating at all - especially about important issues.

### Sloppy Brother

*'I have the responsibility of cleaning up the house before my parents come home from work. After that I'm to start on dinner. My problem is that my messy brother leaves a trail from the time he enters the door. His jacket is hung on the floor, his boots are on the back stairs and he leaves his school books, candy wrappers etc. all over the house. I'm tired of cleaning up after him.'*

Have a talk with your parents and describe the frustration you're having. Your brother should also have responsibilities and one of them should be to pick up after himself. Because he seems to be the one making the most mess, *his* responsibility should be to clean up the house after school, while you start dinner. This way, the chores are allocated fairly.

### No Privacy

*'I'm a very private person. I spend most of my day at work with many people and really look forward to some privacy when I get home. My sister is a gregarious person who never shuts up. I must go into my room to get some peace and quiet and even then, she follows me. In the morning, I like solitude and quiet and again she's bubbling over with conversation. I don't want to hurt her feelings or have to find another place to live, but don't know how to broach this problem.'*

This problem often occurs in family situations where people are *"locked-in"* with other family members. Everyone in this situation must compromise and let others know how they feel. Talking this out calmly is the key to this problem. Be direct and ask your sister what she believes will be a suitable solution to this problem. She might be suffering too, because she may need more socialising during her non-working hours.

People sometimes choose the wrong kind of working environment. Both of you should examine the jobs you have. If you work with many other people and you're essentially a loner, you may be in the wrong type of job for you. On the other hand, if your sister seeks conversation after work, she may not meet this need at her place of employment.

## Morning/Night People

*'My roommate (my brother Bob) is a night owl, watches television until the wee hours of the night - then sleeps in. I'm asleep by ten-thirty most nights and am up at dawn. How can we adjust our schedules to accommodate us both?'*

You'll both have to adjust; especially being quiet while the other person is sleeping. For some, changing roommates is the only viable solution.

Before choosing a roommate you both should have identified this as a possible problem.

## Chronic Fatigue Syndrome

*'My brother has just been diagnosed with chronic fatigue syndrome. I feel terrible - I treated him as if he was lazy and kept after him to become more active. I should have known he was sick – he'd always been so active before he got sick. What signs should I have noticed and how can I help him through this illness.'*

Chronic Fatigue Syndrome (CFS) is a physical illness that strikes people of all ages, ethnic and socio-economic groups and affects one to two per cent of the population. It's about three times more common in women. Unfortunately, ninety percent of patients have not been diagnosed and are not receiving proper medical care for their illness. Despite intensive decade-long research, the cause of this malady remains unknown. Many different viruses, bacterium, toxins and psychological causes have been considered and rejected, but the search continues.

Common symptoms are:

Fatigue, substantial impairment of short-term memory or concentration, sore throat, tender lymph nodes, muscle and joint pain, headaches, ineffective night's sleep and fatigue lasting more than twenty-four hours following exertion.

CFS is diagnosed when these symptoms persist for more than six months and cannot be explained by any other medical or psychological condition.

Treatment is usually aimed at symptom relief. No single therapy exists to help all patients. Treatment must be carefully tailored to meet the needs of each patient. Sleep disorders, pain, gastro-intestinal difficulties, allergies and depression are some of the symptoms that physicians commonly attempt to relieve using prescription and over-the-counter medications. Persons with this illness may have unusual responses to medications, so extremely low dosages should be tried first and gradually increased as appropriate.

Only one drug, Ampligen, is nearing the end of FDA's approval process. Test groups are not receiving and testing this drug. Lifestyle changes, including increased rest, reduced stress, dietary restrictions, nutritional supplementation and minimal exercise are frequently recommended. Supportive therapy, such as counselling, can also help to identify and develop effective coping strategies.

One sign of this disease is an intolerance of previously well-tolerated levels of physical activity. Most patients' symptoms worsen severely, sometimes for days, following even minor exertion. Physicians recommend that they perform limited (and preferably anaerobic or light weight training) and that they listen to their bodies and not push them beyond their limits.

The course of this illness varies greatly. Some recover. Others go between periods of relatively good health and illness and some gradually worsen over time. Others either become worse or better while some improve gradually, but never fully recover. The greatest chance of recovery appears to be within the first five years of the illness, although some may recover at any stage. Those with sudden onset, reported recovery nearly twice as often as those with gradual onset.

So, the bottom line is to have sympathy for what he's going through and help him deal with the frustrations and symptoms that go along with this baffling disease.

## *No time for ME*

*'My sister Marcie and I are both single parents who live together in a home with our children. We have no problem handling time management at work, but we're having problems handling it at home. How can we spend our weekends having some fun for a change?'*

Life runs smoothly at the office, but why does it fall apart at home? Where's the gas bill? When is Sally's next dentist appointment? What groceries do I have to pick up on my way home from work? When you have a dual lifestyle balancing a career and home duties - it's usually the home front that causes grief. Learn to use business techniques in the home as well.

Planning is essential to getting your homemaking chores under control. Use lists for everything; for groceries and tasks that need doing around the home and yard (and who should do them!). Set priorities. Is it more important to have a spotless house or to spend an hour teaching your daughter how to knit? Know the activities that are important to you and what you can let slide, when more important priorities come along.

Your lists should be divided into:

> Have to: (Priority As)
> Need to: (Priority Bs)
> Hope to: (Priority Cs)
> Don't have to: (Priority Ds)

You also need to find time for yourself. This is the area that's usually low on the list of priorities, but, should be near the top. Wise parents (especially single parents) learn that they must be what they might term as *"selfish"*. They plan special activities for themselves, so they can be more effective people. Putting themselves as number one in their priorities, is *not* a sin - it's a necessity (providing they don't take it to excess).

Delegate jobs to your family members. The adults in the home shouldn't do all the chores. An essential ingredient of delegation is follow-up. This will ensure that your children properly complete their tasks. Be sure to give praise for a job well done and help them to improve the quality of their performance. Plan what you'll do if they don't complete their tasks properly. Be consistent with discipline and fair to all members of your family.

When cooking, make multiple batches - it takes just a little longer to make meals for four days than for one. Use your freezer as much as possible. Stop wasting your time picking up groceries every second day - make fewer trips.

Some families leave most of the family chores until the weekend, but then find that their family doesn't have time to do fun activities together. One woman does her shopping Thursday evening, does a batch of wash every day (while preparing and cleaning up from dinner). This eliminates the six batches of wash she used to do every Saturday.

Hire a student (or your children) to do those jobs that pile up such as cutting the grass, painting the fence, shovelling the driveway, helping with the spring cleaning.

In the summer, consider hiring a *"mother's helper"* so that s/he can accomplish babysitting and home care together. Leave *"chore lists"* for your children of what you expect them to do during the day while you're at work. Make them feel part of a team - that they're contributing something valuable to the family unit. Plan special treats to reward good performance.

Try all the above and see if you don't find activities run more smoothly around your home and you have more time for yourselves.

### Expects Favours

'*My brother expects me to drive him everywhere but doesn't offer to pay for the gas. How can I get him to pay his share?*'

Using feedback; let him know how much this annoys you. Tell him what you feel would be a fair contribution on his part towards gas and car expenses. Refuse to drive him unless he contributes to the costs.

### Borrowing Money

'*My sister is always borrowing money from me and seldom pays it back. How can I refuse her request for more money?*'

Explain that she already owes you too much money (have it all itemized) and you can't think of lending her any more until she pays back the existing debt. Decide when she *will* be paying back what she owes, giving deadlines and don't lend her more money until she pays her existing debt.

*'My sister is always borrowing my clothes but doesn't return them the way she receives them.'*

*'My brothers are always lending lawnmowers, tools and equipment and I have to ask for them back.'*

Use feedback to explain how you feel about their behaviour:

### Describe their behaviour:

*'They're borrowing items and aren't returning them properly.'*

### How you felt when they acted that way:

*'You feel they're taking advantage of you.'*

### The Solution:

*'Their friendship is too important to you to jeopardise it by lending them more of your belongings.'*

Remain firm - don't waver.

### Tantrums

*'My brother Bruce continues to have tantrums even as an adult. I can see that this is causing him problems at work and at home with his family. His tantrums include throwing inanimate objects. I've seen the terror in his children's eyes when he does this. What can I do to make him see how destructive this behaviour is to everyone around him?'*

In this case, it's possible that your brother's behaviour is a sign of wife or child abuse. You cannot stand by and let this continue. Talk to his wife to see if your findings are true. If they are, provide the help the wife and children will likely need to deal with the problem. Encourage your brother to obtain professional help to deal with his outbursts.

If you examine the situation and find that your brother isn't abusing his children intentionally, wait until he calms down, then explain how you perceive his behaviour, how it's affecting others and what you'd like him to do to change his behaviour.

Say. *'Bruce, I'd like to talk to you about something that you're doing that upsets me. Is this a good time to talk about it?'*

If he agrees to listen to you say, *'This morning you had a temper tantrum where you ended up throwing the telephone book at the wall. Have you any idea how your actions make your children feel?'*

Then explain how you felt when he acted that way. *'I was watching your children and saw the look of terror in their eyes. To be truthful, I didn't know what to expect from you either because you were out of control.'*

You suggest a solution - *'In the future, could you walk away from situations when you find yourself getting that steamed up? You should consider getting counselling for anger management, so you can control your temper.'*

You might ask him what he was hoping to accomplish with his behaviour. Refuse to give him special treatment to shut him up. The consequences of a repeated performance could be that you'll encourage his wife and children to seek help.

Adults, who still resort to temper tantrums, haven't grown up. These people love the control and power they have over others and enjoy watching everyone jump to do their bidding. This behaviour often allows them to get exactly *what they want* but often results in retaliation from others. Someone who's angry is looking for a good fight and you simply can't buy into it. Other tactics you can use to deal with a person who uses emotional explosions to manipulate you:

    a) Keep your cool and be firm. If the person continues arguing, explain that you're leaving to give him or her time to calm down. Then walk away.

    b) After s/he's more rational, ask for facts about the problem.

    c) Listen carefully and then do what you can to resolve the problem.

    d) S/he may regret his or her outburst. Be ready to deal with the person's guilt feelings.

### *'Aggressive Female' Label*

*'My brother Ted accused me of being an "aggressive female". I've recently been to an assertiveness training course and am changing my usual passive behaviour and am trying to be more assertive. I'm confused about the boundaries between assertive and aggressive behaviour. Could he be right; am I an `aggressive female?'*

This often happens to those (both male and female) who have attended assertiveness training classes. Those who normally associate with them are comfortable with their passive behaviour where they found little resistance to what *they* want to do. When these passive people start asserting their right to have their own opinions, others might erroneously label their behaviour as aggressive. Only if you were imposing your wishes and needs on others, could your behaviour be considered aggressive.

### Poor Listener

*'My brother Phil drives me bananas because I have to repeat almost everything I say to him. He's a very intense person and is normally thoughtful. It's not that he doesn't hear me, because I use the same volume of voice when I repeat my message. How can I get him to stop this habit, because he must be using it with others as well?'*

If he's an intense kind of person, who's distracted with his thoughts, it might take him a bit to re-channel his thinking. One way to approach this problem is to explain to him what his actions are doing to you.

*'Phil, do you realise that lately I've had to repeat almost everything I've said to you? I know you've heard me, because I use the same volume of voice when I repeat myself. I get the feeling that you don't think what I have to say is important. This concerns me, not only because it affects me, but because you're probably doing it to others as well. Do you have any idea why this is happening?'*

This will start a dialogue that should result in an improvement in Phil's listening skills.

### Repetitive Phrases

*'My brother Mark is driving me crazy because he has certain phrases that he repeats – again and again! The particular phrases that bother me the most are, 'You know... all right... okay... and, now...' Once I was listening to him talk on the phone and I counted the times he said 'You know.' In twenty minutes, he repeated the phrase fifty-three times!'*

It's easy to slip into having voice patterns that are very hard to correct. Try saying, *'Mark, I have something to tell you that you may not want to hear, but if I didn't care about you, I'd never bring it up. Do you mind a little constructive criticism?'* (Try this opening phrase whenever you want to give constructive criticism.)

If he agrees (probably reluctantly) continue, *'Mark, when you talked to Ken on the phone yesterday, in twenty minutes, I counted the times you said, "You know" and you said it fifty-three times! You're probably not aware of how often you use this and other phrases, but I imagine it bothers other people as much as it bothers me. Do you have any idea how you got into this habit?'*

If nothing else, this will start a conversation about the problem. If he agrees there's a problem, you might remind him of the problem by having a symbol you can use when he uses the phrases. For example, holding up your hand showing three fingers if he repeats a phrase, three times.

### Mumbler

*'My brother mumbles when he speaks. Everyone is forced to ask him to repeat what he's talking about. This becomes annoying after a while, because everyone must pay such close attention to what he's saying. He doesn't have a speech impediment - he just mumbles all his words together.'*

People do mumble. They fail to a-r-t-i-c-u-l-a-t-e their words, so their words run together. This is a shame, because they're going to be communicating with others the rest of their lives. If mumblers have problems being understood, it certainly seems worthwhile for them to take steps to improve this skill; otherwise they're allowing themselves to remain handicapped in one of the most important communication skills of all; speaking.

Your brother can improve his speaking ability by joining a Toastmasters club or by taking a public speaking course. He'll learn breath control, how to project his voice and how to speak clearly when he talks. Here's a test he can give himself to see whether he's a good speaker or not:

### Rate your Speaking Skills

Rate yourself (or have a friend help you) using the following scale:

**5= Always**
**4= Almost always**
**3= Sometimes**
**2= Rarely**
**1= Never**

1. If I were a listener, would I listen to myself?
2. If I'm being misunderstood, I remember that it's my responsibility to help the other person understand me.
3. I keep my instructions to others short, sweet and to the point.

4. I am aware of when my audience has tuned me out.
5. I make sure my listeners know what I want from them.
6. When I give instructions, I ask for feedback and paraphrasing to make sure I'm understood.
7. I make sure my non-verbal signals (body language, tone of voice, etc.) are the same as my verbal ones.
8. I make sure I don't intimidate my listeners with a loud voice, threatening appearance, intense or prolonged eye contact, verbal attacks, etc.
9. I articulate clearly.
10. I try to use language the listener can understand.

**Total**:

*Scoring:*

40 or more - You're an excellent speaker!
32 – 39 - You're better than average.
25 – 31 - You require improvement.
24 or less- You're not an effective speaker. You need practice, practice and more practice!

Did he chuckle to himself when completing the first question? Did he find there was an element of truth to the question? If so, it's possible that he fit into one of three categories of people who believe they're not worth listening to:

a) He has trouble getting his words out. He knows what he wants to say but can't quite say it (because he lacks verbal fluency). Verbal fluency enables us to express our thoughts clearly, so others understand exactly what we mean.
b) He's not up on what's going on in the world. Often people insulate themselves from the terrible situations that are going on in the world. Suddenly, in social situations they may find they don't know what's going on. Therefore, they might feel they have nothing to contribute to the conversation. The solution is to catch up on what's happening.
c) It's possible that he runs off at the mouth, has problems keeping conversations short, sweet and to the point. He needs to spend time organising his thoughts before he speaks. He can practice by writing down his thoughts or use a tape recorder to catch himself.

Then he can practice re-arranging his words using more precise language until he can say what he wants to say without rambling.

### *Promises, Promises*

*'I have a sister who promises she will do something and then lets me down. I don't think she does it on purpose, but she does it often. I want to keep her as a friend but get so exasperated with her; I don't talk to her for a week.'*

When she says she'll do something for you, give her the chance to back out of the arrangement by stating, *'I'm counting on you to do this for me. If you feel you can't, please let me know now, otherwise I'll be very disappointed.'* If she does let you down use feedback:

### Describe her behaviour:
*'You didn't pick me up after work and I waited for half an hour for you before I took a bus home.'*

### How you felt when she acted that way:
*'I was very hurt that you didn't think enough of me to let me know you wouldn't be coming.'*

### What you feel would be the solution:
*'I'll need a promise from you that in the future you'll call me if you have to change your plans.'*

### *Uninvited children*

*'I'm planning my wedding and want to make it clear to those I've invited to the wedding reception, that I don't want them to bring their children. This would include my brother's children, who are very unruly. Several of my friends have allowed children at their wedding receptions and it was chaos with cranky, misbehaved children taking over the evening.'*

You have every right to eliminate children from your reception if you wish to do so. On your R.S.V.P. card, have the words *'No children please.'* Emphasise this by writing the name of the people who *are* invited to the reception dinner on the reply card.

*'My wife and I enjoy entertaining our families. We have grown children, but our brothers and sisters still have young families. I find these evenings to be very stressful to my wife and me because they don't understand that we've invited <u>them</u> for the evening, not their entire family. How can I be tactful when I invite them in the future?'*

Be direct and tell them that your gathering is adults only. You might contemplate the idea of having another family gathering in the future (an afternoon barbecue possibly) where their children would be welcome.

### Summer visitors

*'My brother and his family came for a visit last summer and I've hardly spoken to him and his wife since. My wife and I went to a lot of trouble to rent a houseboat and I took my motorboat along, so we could water ski. Nothing seemed to impress them and all I heard about was what was wrong with everything. There were too many bugs, the water was too cold, it rained one day, etc.*

*'And their daughter! She drove us crazy with her whining about everything. She fought with our son, interrupted our conversations at every turn and tried to be the centre of everyone's attention. What a drag! What a holiday!*

*'They knew all about our plans before they came and seemed to be as excited as we were at the prospect of having so much fun. What could we have done differently to ensure we all had a good holiday?'*

Summer visitors should accept hospitality graciously and adapt to the ways of the household. Unfortunately, relatives sometimes behave differently than non-relatives and take advantage of their hosts.

When things started to go awry, you should have sat down with your brother and said, *'It appears that I was wrong in thinking you'd like the holiday we planned. I can't do much about the bugs, the cold water and the rain. What could I be doing to make this a happy holiday for you that I'm not doing right now?'*

This will start the dialogue at least and let your brother know that the situation with the environment is out of your control. Then, bring up the situation of the child's behaviour. Make sure your son is not causing his cousin to be miserable.

If you've assured yourself that this is not the case, say, *'I find that I get annoyed at Sarah because of her constant interruptions to our conversations. I can't finish a sentence before she's interrupting me with her whining. What do you think would make her happier and less likely to use such disruptive behaviour?'*

Your brother might not be happy about the conversation, but he can't deny that what you say is true if you point it out to him. Because of the cramped quarters on the houseboat, this kind of behaviour from the child would make everyone feel as if they were in jail. They couldn't get away from her whining. You had to say something for your sanity if for nothing else!

### Babysitting

*'I babysit my sister's children three days a week while she's at a part-time job. Every work day is a scramble for her and she's always rushing off for work because she's so late dropping them off. It's getting her two and four-year-olds ready in the morning that seems to be the problem. They dawdle, complaining about what they're going to wear and what they're having for breakfast. She doesn't seem to know how to settle this.'*

Here are some tips you can pass on to her:

1.   The night before, she should put out two outfits each for the children to wear. They choose which of the two outfits they wear - no exceptions and set a reasonable time limit for them to finish dressing.
2.   Have shoes with Velcro fasteners so they can put them on themselves.
3.   No breakfast until the child is dressed. If they're late - take breakfast to the babysitters.
4.   Once a month as a treat for good behaviour - take them out for breakfast or stop and get breakfast to take to the babysitters to eat.
5.   Have coats and boots on hooks for easy access.
6.   No TV in the morning!
7.   If they misbehave in the morning, she would explain the consequences of their behaviour and be sure to follow-through. This could be that they won't have a bedtime story that night or she would remove some other treat they normally have.

### Body Odour

Larry explained his problem, *'My brother Wally has body odour that is so strong, that I hate being around him. The other evening, my wife and I, Wally and his new girlfriend were out for an evening. His girlfriend approached me because she had noticed the body odour too and had asked me to talk to Wally about it. How can I approach this problem without causing dissention between us?'*

Larry had several choices on how he could deal with this problem. He could ask the girlfriend to do it herself, talk to his parents about it or could do it himself.

He decided to speak directly to Wally and started the conversation by saying, *'Wally, I have something I want to talk to you about. I hope you realise that I'd never do anything to hurt your feelings or embarrass you, but because I'm not only your brother, but consider myself a close friend, there's something you should know.'*

He watched Wally's body language to see if his statement upset or angered him. Wally appeared interested in what he had to say, rather than angry. Larry continued, *'This conversation is as painful for me, as it is for you. I know you're not aware of it, but you have a problem with body odour. I thought you'd rather know about it, than have me ignore the situation and have it cause you problems with others.'*

Wally blushed and looked down. He explained, *'I didn't know it was that bad. I've been going to a doctor for a foot odour problem. I guess the medicine I'm using isn't helping. I'll make another appointment this afternoon. Thanks for letting me know about this.'*

This was an embarrassing conversation for both brothers, but Larry cared enough about his brother to let him know there was a problem and Wally was mature enough to take the constructive criticism.

It's interesting to note that women have lower odour *"thresholds"*, meaning they can detect fainter odours than men and are often offended by body odour long before a man is even aware of the odour.

### Obese Sister

*'My sister is very obese. As if that wasn't bad enough – she smells. She tries to cover up the odour with perfume, but it doesn't mask the smell at all.'*

Use the same tactics that Larry used with his brother. You should also express your concerns about her weight problem and try to give her the support she may need to get her weight down. The key here - is to show concern – not censure. She doesn't need more criticism – she needs support to help her overcome these two serious problems.

What is the difference between naturally thin people and fat ones? Thin people eat when they're hungry and stop when they're full. It seems so basic, this thing called eating. But obesity experts say many weight problems are simply a matter of losing touch with internal clues. People eat when they're not hungry and continue way beyond the point where they're full. Non-hunger eating is one of the most difficult addictions people must deal with. Everyone eats too much sometimes. But people who constantly try to control their eating (rather than base it on hunger) run into trouble.

Unfortunately, well-meaning parents feed their infant until all the cereal is gone, prod their toddler to finish the chicken whether he's still hungry or not and urge their children to clean their plates *"or else"*. These parents are messing up hunger signals for their children.

The first step for her to take is to be mindful when she's eating - to focus on the food and remove distractions such as television, books or the telephone. Have her write down what she's feeling when she's eating. She'll soon realise that most of the time *"hunger"* will not appear on her list.

Does your sister have problems controlling her weight or find her weight fluctuates so much that she's resorted to wearing sweat pants or garments with elastic waist bands? If so - she's just sabotaged her efforts to keep her weight down. How do I know this? Because it happened to me!

I'd always been a lightweight - the envy of my friends. I could eat anything, anytime and never appear to gain weight. I seemed to have a shut-off valve that told me emphatically that I was full - many times before the food on my plate was finished. I simply felt too full to eat another mouthful and remain comfortable. My fast metabolism obviously helped me, and I scoffed at the idea that I could gain weight just like everyone else. What a dreamer I turned out to be!

I'd been offering seminars in Hawaii for three weeks and decided that since it was December I'd treat myself, by extending my visit to seven weeks. Like the natives, I *"hung loose"*, wearing mostly bathing suits, shorts and slacks with elastic waistbands or sweats when it was cooler. I even bought a loose-fitting Hawaiian dress that had no discernible waist at all.

You know the result. After returning home and trying to get into my regular clothes I realised I'd gained eight kilos (about fifteen pounds)! How could this have happened to me? I didn't think I'd eaten more than usual, so tried to figure out what had happened to change things. I soon realised that one of my major deterrents to excessive eating was that I physically felt too full to eat more. I felt full because my waistband would tighten as I consumed my meal - sometimes making me feel uncomfortable if I ate even one more mouthful.

It's likely that your sister would feel the same way too, if she had a waistband to remind her that she's full. She would start by getting outfits that have rigid waistbands. Then, instead of loosening that button on her waistband during her meal - she would push herself away from the table (leaving the excess food on her plate). She should never feel as if she *must* finish everything. Her parents might have when she was young - but that doesn't apply now. It's those extra bites she takes *after* she's full - that put on the pounds.

Obesity plus stress equals trouble. Men with beer bellies and women with apple-shaped bodies have a high chance of developing diabetes. Many may not even know they have it, because there often are no symptoms. Doctors addressing a symposium on diabetes drove home the point that fat and diabetes often go together. One doctor stated, *'If you're a diabetic and especially one who's overweight, you can sign your death certificate today, but just can't put a date on it.'*

While there are few symptoms, a diabetic who develops hyperglycaemia (too high a level of glucose in the blood) may have great thirst and hunger, a dry mouth and a need to urinate often. We don't completely understand the cause, but anyone with at least one close relative with diabetes inherits the tendency to get it.

Eighty per cent of diabetics will die of cardio-vascular disease. A greater number stand the risk of going blind (accounts for half of blindness under age 65 and one-quarter of visual impairment). Forty per cent of amputations (because of poor circulation) are due to diabetes. Diabetes is a lifelong disorder in which the body can't properly store and provide fuel to cells. Either the pancreas doesn't produce enough insulin, so the body can use glucose (or sugar) for energy or it's unable to use the insulin it does produce.

Doctors noted that some obese diabetics have cured themselves by losing weight, maintaining a low-fat diet, exercising, quitting smoking and reducing alcohol consumption. Unfortunately, other doctors endorse the use of artificial sweeteners as did diabetes organisations that recommend these diet products to people who desperately need to lose weight; even though it has been amply documented that the formaldehyde in aspartame (an artificial sweetener) stores in fat cells, particularly on the hips and thighs and is then difficult - sometimes impossible to dislodge. The most insidious thing about aspartame is that it is addictive and has serious withdrawal effects.

*'My little sister is nine and weighs 62 kilos (approximately 140 pounds). All she does is sit around and watch television and eat junk food. How can I make my parents deal with this – I'm ashamed of her gluttony.'*

Instead of concentrating only on her diet - it's important that she gets up off that couch and exercises. Your sister could be a prime candidate for osteoporosis when she's a senior (if she lives that long). Young girls who begin exercising before puberty may be drastically improving their bone strength as adults. Researchers examined young tennis and squash players - comparing bone length in the playing arm to that of their other bones. The scientists hoped to answer questions about the importance of building mineral mass in growing bones just before puberty.

Bone mass usually rises dramatically just before menarche - peaks in the late teens - and then begins a gradual lifelong decline. Girls who began playing before menarche had about twice the build-up of bone strength in their playing arms as girls who began playing later. The study provides evidence that physical activity during the pubescent years is crucial for maximising bone mass.

I can verify this research because of my own personal experience. Several years ago, I wanted to check my bone density because I was concerned that because of my busy life, I might be putting myself in jeopardy by lifting heavy suitcases when I travel. I made an appointment and just after the technician had completed my scan she asked me, *'Do you exercise much?'* I sheepishly admitted that I didn't as much as I used to, but had a busy, active life. I asked her if there was a problem, but she said my doctor would have to discuss my bone scan with me personally.

After a bit of uneasy time, I finally spoke with my doctor who told me that I had the highest bone density scan that had come through her clinic! We then tried to determine why my bone density was so high. We discussed my diet and I had to admit that I didn't drink much milk but enjoyed having a piece of cheese or a handful of peanuts for a snack at night. We both agreed that my diet wasn't exceptional. Then we discussed the amount of exercise I did. I guiltily admitted that I didn't spend much more than about an hour a week exercising.

*'Well, something's given you this exceptional bone density.'* We were finally able to determine that it was the exercise I had done as a pre-pubescent child. From when I was eight until I was fourteen - I had trained three times a week - for two hours at a time for the Canadian Olympics in swimming. So, you see - if you have young *"couch potatoes"* (male or female) in your home - you're allowing them to set themselves up for low bone density when they mature.

Be sure to show your parents this information and urge them to get her up and moving before it's too late for her bones to develop properly.

### Suicide

*'I'm concerned about my teen-aged brother. He's been so depressed lately, that I'm concerned that he's contemplating suicide. How can I help him?'*

Suicide is common among teenagers. Nineteen percent of teens admit they've thought of suicide with twenty-two of them attempting to kill themselves. Most depressed teens don't tell anyone about his or her despair. Almost two-thirds - sixty-three percent of the thirteen- to eighteen-year-olds said embarrassment, fear and peer pressure and the stigma surrounding mental illness, kept them from seeking help.

Children who grow up in families touched by violence, mental illness or divorce have higher rates of depression than the general population. Experts say that sometimes restoring normal brain-chemical balances with medication can be used in the treatment of some depression. High-income earners report less depression - but higher stress levels. The amount of daylight can affect some (the winter blues). This problem is often treated with artificial sun stimuli.

Signs of depression that can often lead to suicide are:
a) Feelings of sadness or irritability;
b) Loss of interest in activities the person once enjoyed;
c) Changes in weight or appearance;
d) Changes in sleeping pattern;
e) Feelings of guilt, hopelessness or worthlessness;
f) Inability to concentrate, remember things or make decisions;
g) Fatigue or loss of energy;
h) Restlessness;
i) Complaints of physical aches and pains for which no medical explanation can be found;

77

j)   Giving away of possessions; and
k)   Getting their lives in order.

There are many myths about suicide:

1.   **Myth**: People who talk about suicide don't tend to kill themselves. They just want attention.
     **Fact**: More than 70 percent of those who attempt or complete suicide, previously threatened to take their lives.

2.   **Myth**: Those who do complete suicide rarely warn others.
     **Fact:** Eight of ten individuals who kill themselves left clues, although they're not always verbal and may be hard to detect.

3.   **Myth**: It's better not to mention suicide to a severely depressed person, because it will give them ideas.
     **Fact:** Many depressed persons have already thought of suicide as a way out and discussing it openly can help them sort through their problems, bringing relief and understanding.

Talk to your brother's family doctor and ask for a referral to a counsellor who can help him. Then accompany him to his counselling session and give him the moral and emotional support he will need to deal with his situation. With his permission, talk to other family members to ensure that they too can help him through his crisis and support him during his time of need.

Here are other ways your brother can help himself deal with the tensions in life:

*The Canadian Mental Health Association supplied the following information.*

**Talk it out:**

When something is worrying you - talk it out. Sit down with a level-headed person you trust; husband or wife, father or mother, good friend, clergyman, family doctor, teacher, school counsellor. Talking helps to relieve strain and enables you to see the problem more clearly.

**Escape for a while:**

Often it helps to escape from the problem for a short time; lose yourself in a movie or book, take a drive in the country. It's realistic to escape punishment long enough to recover breath and balance but be prepared to come back and grapple with the problem when you're more composed.

## Work off your anger:

While anger may give you a temporary sense of righteousness or even power, it will probably leave you feeling foolish. If you have the urge to lash out, wait until tomorrow. Do something constructive with that pent-up energy – spade the garden, clean out the garage, play a game of tennis, take a long walk. A day or two later you'll be better prepared to deal with the problem.

## Give in occasionally:

If you find yourself getting into frequent quarrels and feeling defiant, remember that frustrated children behave the same way. Stand your ground but do it calmly and remember that you *could* be wrong. Even if you're dead right, it's easier on your system to give in now and then. You'll relieve some tension and have a feeling of satisfaction.

## Do something for others:

If you find that you're worrying about *yourself* all the time, try doing something for someone else. The steam will go out of your worries and instead, you'll have a good feeling.

## Take one thing at a time:

For people under tension, an ordinary workload may seem unbearable. The tasks loom so large that it becomes painful to tackle any part. To sort your way out of it, take a few of the most urgent tasks and pitch into them. Leave everything else aside. Once you've cleared a few away, the others won't seem such a *"horrible mess"*. You'll be into the swing and the balance of the work will go more easily.

## Shun the 'super person' role:

Some people expect too much of themselves; they strive for perfection in everything they do. The frustration of failure leaves them in a constant state of worry and anxiety. Decide what you do well and put your major effort in this direction. These are probably things you like to do, hence ones that give you the most satisfaction. Then, perhaps, tackle the ones you can't do so well. Give them your best, but don't berate yourself if you don't achieve the impossible.

**Go easy with your criticism:**

Expecting too much of others can lead to feelings of frustration and disappointment. Each person has his or her own virtues, shortcomings and values - his own right to develop as an individual. Instead of being critical, search out the other's good points and help him or her to develop them. This will give you both satisfaction and help you gain a better perspective of yourself.

**Give the other person a break:**

People under emotional tension often feel they must *"get there first"* – to edge out the other person. It can be something as common as highway driving. Competition is contagious, but so is co-operation. When you give the others a break, you often make things easier for yourself; if they no longer feel *you* are a threat to them, they stop being a threat to *you*.

**Make yourself 'available.'**

Many of us have the feeling that we're being left out, slighted, neglected and rejected. Often, we just imagine that other people feel this way about us. They may be waiting for us to make the first move. Instead of shrinking away and withdrawing, it's much healthier to continue *to "make yourself available"*. Of course, the opposite - pushing yourself forward at every opportunity – is equally futile. This can be misinterpreted and lead to real rejection. There is a middle ground. Try it.

**Schedule your recreation.**

Some people drive themselves so hard that they allow themselves almost no time for recreation - an essential for good physical and mental health. Set aside definite hours for hobby or sport that will absorb you completely; a time to forget about your work and worries.

## *Perfectionist*

*'My sister Jennie is a perfectionist, not only at work, but in her apartment as well. How can I get her to understand that everything doesn't have to be perfect and it's okay to let some tasks go? I find that she's refusing to go out with her friends because 'I have too much to do at home tonight.' She hasn't learned to relax and let unimportant tasks slide.'*

Jennie probably feels guilty if she's not working. Ask her if this is true in her case. Help her get time management help. This will enable her to set priorities on what's important to her. Explain (more than once if necessary) that everything doesn't have to be perfect in her apartment. Hopefully, you can help re-channel Jennie's energy towards having more fun. Life's too short to spend it just existing - Jennie needs to live a little and stop *to "smell the flowers"* without feeling guilty. Regularly, invite her to parties and events, so she can change her routine.

### Dishonest Sibling

*'My brother Steve and I had a falling out five years ago and I've hardly spoken to him since. Our disagreement relates to the settlement of my father's estate. Everything my father owned went to my mother (as it should have). Shortly after, when our mother was diagnosed as having Alzheimer's disease, we made a careful accounting of her assets.*

*Our parents were very generous to my brother, my sister and me. They would lend money to us interest free. In return they expected us to pay back the money within a reasonable length of time. When we borrowed money, we'd give our parents a promissory note and as we paid off our loans, they would destroy the documents.*

*The problem began when each of us explained what we still owed our parents at the time of my father's death. My sister Ann and I were doing quite well financially and had paid off all our promissory notes. Steve was heavily in debt. He had borrowed almost two hundred thousand dollars from our parents for two separate mortgages. We went through the contents of my parent's safety-deposit box but couldn't find promissory notes for his mortgages. Because Steve lives in the same city as my parents, he had earlier access to their safety-deposit box. He explained that the money my parents had loaned him for his mortgages had been "gifts".'*

*Ann and I know this can't be true because of the history with our parents. Because there is no legal paperwork (except the promissory notes my parents drew up), we can't prove that he did owe this money.*

*My mother isn't suffering financially. Her estate presently amounts to about one hundred thousand dollars. That isn't the issue. The issue is that I can't forgive him for being so dishonest and taking the money that should rightfully belong to our mother. I keep reminding myself that life is short and that I should make up with him. I don't think I can forgive him for this breach of trust - especially with those who trusted him implicitly - his own parents.'*

When faced with this type of problem, it's important to write down all the possible solutions to it. Then identify the advantages and disadvantages of each way and choose the best solution for you. In the above situation, there are so many factors involved which must be taken into consideration such as: What will happen when your mother dies and the three of you divide her estate? Could this conflict resurface at what could be a very traumatic time in your life? Would it be better to get the problem solved now when there is not a death involved?

One solution would be to break the ice with Steve and discuss your mother's estate. Get your sister Ann involved. You both could explain how you feel about the money you believe he still owes your mother. Offer alternatives to him. Suggest that he repay your mother the money he owes or have him agree (in writing) that he wouldn't receive any of her estate when she dies. Tell him that he's already received more than double what both you and Ann would receive upon the death of your mother. If he disagrees, ask him to explain why he believes he deserves more of your parent's estate than you and Ann do.

If you can't resolve the situation, you'll have to judge whether you want to continue communicating with Steve and if you'll take the matter to court now. There might be a record of payments he made to them before your father died. He would have to explain why he had made those payments to your parents. In the meantime, you'll have given him ample opportunity to settle the matter. You may have to resort to taking the matter to probate court after your mother dies, so the estate is divided equally.

*'Steve and I haven't spoken for five years since he cheated on our parents. That I don't miss, but I do miss seeing his daughter (my niece) and since he has custody of her he keeps me from seeing her.'*

Your niece must visit her mother occasionally (unless he has sole custody). Talk to her mother and ask if you could be there the next time your niece visits her mother. You will likely have to explain to her mother why you're requesting this visit.

### Mental/Physical Abuse

*'My sister is being mentally and physically abused by her husband. I can't convince her that she should leave him. How can I help her?'*

Mental abuse often begins when couples *"snipe"* at each other. The more a marriage is in trouble, the more sniping there seems to be. Sniping includes the following:

1.  One partner is telling a story. The other spouse keeps interjecting with corrections of the story.
2.  One partner makes disparaging comments related to the other sex, forcing the partner to defend his/her gender. (i.e.: Women are such awful drivers.)
3.  Start fights in public or in front of friends or family.
4.  Play one-upmanship games or competes openly with his/her partner.
5.  Something went wrong, so it must be because of something the other partner has done (scapegoat and/or passes-the-buck).
6.  Won't admit s/he's wrong even when s/he is.
7.  If his/her partner wins at a game, he or she becomes cranky or sulks.
8.  If his/her partner wants some privacy or space, s/he follows him/her around asking, *'What's wrong'* and won't take the explanation that s/he wants to be alone to think things out.
9.  He or she holds grudges, pouts or gives the other the silent treatment.
10. Makes cutting or sarcastic remarks.
11. Makes fun of how his/her partner looks, what he or she wears or things s/he does.
12. Digs up old problems and indiscretions and won't let go of past arguments.
13. He or she blames others for how s/he feels, making comments such as:
    *'Now look what you made me do!'*
    *'He always makes me feel so inferior.'*
    *'She makes me so mad when she...'*
14. (Blaming his/her partner for causing his/her bad behaviour).

The best way to help your sister if she's being emotionally or physically abused is to:

*   Let her know that *you* know there's something wrong and that you care. Put the emphasis on your own fears: *'I'm afraid that you are caught in an abusive relationship and I'm worried about your safety.'*
*   Let her know you believe the things she tells you.
*   Don't get discouraged if she refuses to leave the relationship or denies the abuse. Statistics show that women are abused on

average thirty-five times before the violence is reported - and leave home seven times before they leave for good.

- Supply her with the information from the emergency shelter and let her know there is help available.
- Offer to help and invite her to call at any time of day or night. Tell her you'll drive her to the emergency shelter if she ever decides to go (make sure you know where it is and how to get her there).

Whether it's a family member, co-worker or neighbour, it's never easy to intervene. There's the fear that your suspicions are unfounded or that the woman will deny the abuse. The important thing is to let her know - you know, and you care. Friends and family members sometimes get fed up waiting for the relationship to end. It's important for people to understand there's a head and heart working here. The head says leave, but the heart says stay. It's crucial for friends and family members to be patient. When she's ready, she'll leave.

Unlike child abuse, in many cases there is no legal obligation for anyone to report wife abuse, but police can't help anyone they don't know is being hurt. There's nothing to lose by reporting it, as the call can be kept confidential. Many police departments have a policy of laying charges whenever there is evidence of abuse, with or without the woman's consent. That can help protect the woman from further retaliation from a violent spouse.

You might obtain a copy of my book ***Dealing with Domestic Violence and Child Abuse – Society's Judicial Disgrace!***

### Death of a family member

*'My brother's wife died suddenly in a car accident. Not only is he having a terrible time getting through this - but his children are too. How can I help them?'*

Besides comforting and helping him learn how to take over a household devoid of a wife and mother, there's much you can do to assist with the children. Children who've had a parent die may go into shock. Some deny that their parent is dead or lack signs that express grief. He may not realise these danger signals, but you can watch for the signs. Like adults, children must grieve. Some children feel guilty, possibly because of words they may have exchanged with their mother before she died, or they could feel that somehow that they were responsible for her death. When someone close to a child, dies for some reason the child may feel that *they* made it happen. They need reassurance that they had nothing to do with their mother's illness and death.

Check to see how they're doing at school. Warn the school authorities about the mother's death and ask them to keep your brother informed about any unusual behaviour of the child. If serious problems surface, suggest that your brother ask his clergyman or a psychologist to help both himself and his children deal with their grief. Ask other close relatives (especially motherly women) to spend time with his children to help share their grief and obtain the nurturing they may need to get through the first few months of grieving. Also have him read Betty Jane Wylie's book ***Beginnings: A Book for Widows*** which can help widowers as well.

*'I'm seventeen and my parents have just told me that my five-year-old sister has leukaemia and is not likely to live for more than six months. They're in shock and wonder when and how they can prepare my younger brother and sister (seven and nine years of age) for this eventuality and help them through it all?'*

One of the most difficult roles that come with being a child's caregiver is that of the bearer of bad news when a loved one is sick or dies. For children, the death of a grandparent, classmate and especially a sibling or parent is often traumatic. Death is but another passage in the cycle of life, but when it comes to discussing death with their children, many parents have difficulty finding the right words - and for good reason. Adults don't particularly enjoy thinking about death themselves. That reticence makes discussing the topic with their kids more difficult.

Death can be a subject fraught with mystery, shrouded in uncertainty and full of questions from the children. For that reason, parents need to tackle the subject early on - before the loved one dies. They should deal with it honestly and sensitively and before it arises unexpectedly.

Parents should keep in mind however; younger children may not understand the concepts of heaven and hell and may be unnecessarily frightened. Parents with strong spiritual or religious convictions shouldn't offer involved theological explanations about death; rather their response should be a simple, factual reply. While many parents feel that children under ten are too young to understand death, some experts suggest discussions begin with children as young as three. Young children have a very difficult time learning what death is, because of the abstract nature of the concept. What a three-year-old and a teenager understand are two different things. A person's conception of death evolves as one matures:

Preschool age. Children at this age are primarily concerned with three questions: *'What is death?'* *'What makes people die?'* and *'What happens to people when they die; where do they go?'* They may not grasp the finality of death.

Ages five to nine. These children are better able to understand the meaning of physical death because of their own life experiences. At this stage, youngsters neither deny death nor accept its inevitability.

Ages nine and older. Children at this stage can form realistic concepts based on observation. They understand death's finality and that death is inevitable.

Regardless of the child's age, parents need to start by examining their own beliefs. Before they can talk about death with a child, they need to have a solid grasp on their concept of death. Many mistakenly use words like *"passed away"* or *"departed"*, or expressions such as *'We lost Grandma.'*

While parents believe such words soften the blow - they get in the way of the child's understanding. They need to give the dead a good place to go. When introducing the concept of death to young children, many parents feel good explaining that the dead end up in a pleasant place like heaven. They need to give the child a concept of another place that is considered a safe place for youngsters.

But they mustn't make that paradise sound too tempting. They need to temper their comments so that these children won't do things to get there themselves or contemplate suicide. We need to define death as something that is inevitable, but that they don't take steps to help them get there.

Be aware that the demands on your parents will be so great during your sister's illness, that they won't have much time for you and your siblings. This might make all of you feel neglected or feel jealous because of the attention they'll be giving to your dying sister. This could lead to guilt feelings. Your parents should enlist the help of close friends, teachers and grandparents who can step in to make sure you children have your questions dealt with and feel loved and cared for.

Another real fear your younger siblings might have is that they might catch whatever it is and die too. Because of this, they may be reluctant to come close to your sister. Parents often make the mistake of isolating their children from the sick child, which makes them wonder, *'What's going on that I don't know about.'* Or, *'Is my sister going to make me sick too?'* Other parents smother their remaining children with attention and overprotection.

Your parents need to watch for signs that your brother or sister is in trouble if they start having outbursts of temper or crying either at home or at school. Their grades may start to slip, or the child may skip school.

They could be smouldering cauldrons of anger and guilt or have feelings of abandonment. Some may wish their sibling would die so they can have more attention and then feel guilty because of those awful feelings. It's a trying time for all members of the family, but with enough support from friends and family, they will get through this.

### *Jealousy*

*'My brother is a very jealous man - not only relating to his relationship with his wife - but in other areas of his life. He's jealous when a co-worker gets a promotion and when one of our children graduated from college he sulked for days because neither he nor his siblings had the opportunity to do so. How can I explain how destructive his jealousy has become to his relationships with others?'*

Recent studies show that jealousy strikes women and men equally and probably more often than they want to admit. There are fundamental differences between normal jealousy and the destructive kind. Normal jealousy arises out of a real fear or anticipation of the loss of a valued relationship. It flares up when a threat is perceived and then subsides. Destructive jealousy persists despite the absence of a real or probable threat. Even normal jealousy can become destructive if either person tries to hide it or feels guilty about it. Concealed jealousy is bound to breed resentment, suspicion and a desire for revenge. Ultimately, it can drive a wedge between two individuals. Studies have shown that expressing jealous feelings can be constructive to a relationship by helping to resolve the feelings, rather than letting them fester.

Your brother suffers from jealousy and resentment and cannot accept that others have earned whatever recognition or status they've achieved in life. He likely feels that other's achievements were obtained through *"luck"* and that he's deprived because life hasn't been so kind to him. By putting others down (and making himself feel more important) he tries to discredit others' accomplishments. He may even want revenge and he may vent his frustration on others with hostile acts.

Use feedback to identify what his actions are doing to those around him. Ask him to account for why he has such a jealous nature. Once he's admitted that he has a problem, let him know when his jealousy is rearing its ugly head again. It will help if you encourage him more and give him lots of praise for his own authentic acts. Show interest in him - his goals, ambitions and successes and downplay his perceived failures. He seems to desperately need this kind of approval. When that approval doesn't come his jealousy surfaces. It's likely that he hasn't had much approval for most of his life and craves it from others.

When his jealousy flares up, he should use the incident to explore what is underlying his jealous feelings. For instance, he may be jealous of his partner's business knowledge and associate this with his dissatisfaction with his job. Her enthusiasm for her work may remind him of his own frustrations. He needs to pinpoint what triggers his jealousy, so he can take steps to improve his life. If he's jealous because his wife spends too much time on the phone with friends, he could say, *'I don't really understand why I feel this way, but I get uncomfortable when you talk so much with your friends. Can we talk about it?'*

### Postpartum Depression

*'My sister Caroline is suffering from terrible postpartum depression. I suffered through this myself after I had my first child and remember how awful it was, because nobody helped me through it. What can I do to help her deal with this terrible depression?'*

Being overwhelmed and without energy for the simplest task are symptoms of the profound despair that strikes at least one in ten new mothers. As Caroline explained, *'I feel so ill that I can't function in even the simplest way. I had to hire a woman to come in and help with the children.'*

Using data from more than 35,000 deliveries researchers clearly demonstrate a sevenfold increase in the risk of psychiatric hospitalisation in the first three months after delivery. This significant incidence of depression and the peak in the number of cases diagnosed shortly after delivery makes it clear that the postpartum period is unique in the development of mental illness. Of the millions of births occurring annually, 40 per cent are complicated by some form of a postpartum mood disorder.

Postpartum depression (PPD) usually begins with a milder form of the condition, known as *"maternity blues"* or *"baby blues"* that are experienced by between 40 and 85 per cent of deliveries. Physicians and patients often view it as a *"normal"* phenomenon that usually occurs in the first week to ten days following birth. For most new mothers, the depressed mood, confusion, crying jags, mood swings, sleep and appetite disturbances, anxiety and irritability, which are thought to be caused by a sudden drop in estrogen and progesterone after delivery - gradually go away by themselves.

PPD symptoms can include behavioural changes such as a desire to sleep constantly or insomnia, hopelessness and disinterest in daily life, feelings of deep sadness, mood swings, irritability, extreme anxiety or feelings of being trapped and isolated. Those who don't understand that the condition is a disease affecting brain chemistry have been guilty of suggesting that these mothers probably just need a night out to snap out of it.

At the other end of the spectrum is a comparatively rare disease that affects about .1 to .2 per cent of deliveries. Patients are severely impaired, suffering from hallucinations and delusions that frequently focus on the infant dying or being divine or demonic. These hallucinations often tell the patient to hurt herself or others, placing these mothers at the highest risk for committing infanticide and/or suicide

Between these two extremes is postpartum depression, which is increasingly recognised as a serious complication of childbirth that occurs in 10 - 15 per cent of all deliveries and a staggering 26 to 32 per cent of all adolescent deliveries. More than 60 per cent of patients have an onset of symptoms within the first six weeks postpartum. Most patients suffer from this illness for more than six months and if untreated 25 per cent of patients are still depressed a year later. Four years later approximately 80 per cent of patients sought help again for psychiatric complaints.

These depressed mothers often show a more negative attitude towards their children and many change their future childbearing plans, resorting to adoption, abortion and in some cases even sterilisation.

Health officials are worried that women aren't finding the help that's available to them in the community. The problem is that if these women don't get treatment and support early on, then their depression often gets worse. They might need hospitalisation, their marital relationship or the relationship with their baby and other children can be adversely affected. Studies show that depressed mothers raise depressed babies and this stress can spawn clinically depressed fathers.

But help is at hand. Start by having her contact her family doctor. Go along with her and be supportive. And have her contact a public health nurse to discuss her condition. Many healthcare services have created information packages that are distributed by public health nurses who make home visits immediately after a baby's delivery.

Another health group have all mothers who bring their babies in for their two-month immunisation complete a brief questionnaire designed by psychiatrists to detect postpartum depression. Don't do nothing - make sure she obtains the help she needs to get through this traumatic time.

A lot of women don't realise that it's happening to them, so they don't seek help or if they do - they're hesitant to ask for help. A stigma has long been attached to any form of depression, but new mothers feel doubly threatened because motherhood is commonly thought of as a wonderful experience. Many feel they're a failure because they can't manage as simple a thing as a tiny baby. They're supposed to be happy and have a happy baby, so a lot of women won't reach out for help because they think others will judge them as unfit mothers or even take their babies away. There's incredible societal pressure. Make sure she knows she's not a bad mom - that this isn't her fault and there is treatment for her condition.

### Unemployment

*'Because of the drastic cuts being made in the health-care field, my sister's terrified that her position as a nurse is going to be cut and she'll find herself unemployed. She has admitted that she's tired of nursing but doesn't know what else she can do. She's a single mother with two school-aged. What steps should she be taking to prepare for that eventuality?'*

It's easy to put our heads down, plodding along, doing our job and it's only when that job is pulled out from beneath us that we take stock of where we are. We may find that:

a)  We're afraid to try new ventures – it's much safer staying in the rut we're in.
b)  We don't really like our job - but it's steady and we don't want to *"rock the boat"* by looking elsewhere.
c)  There are far more interesting and exciting jobs we'd like to have, but our families depend upon us to bring in a steady paycheque.

In this tight economy, we all need to prepare ourselves for the possibility that:

1.  We may be laid off from our existing positions.
2.  If we're self-employed, we may find that our product or service is not bringing in enough revenue for us to survive (at least temporarily).

When we analyse our usage of time, most of us spend ten hours (and sometimes more) of every working day, getting ready for, travelling to and working at our jobs. The average man works forty-five years before retirement. Women spend an average of thirty-five years working either part- or full-time in the paid workforce before retirement. Doesn't it make sense for us to be spending these valuable years performing work we enjoy?

Many positions will become redundant. Most clerical jobs have ceased to exist because their supervisors and managers are conducting business via their computers. If she's *"put all her eggs in one basket"* (has worked in only one occupation) now is the time for her to prepare for the future, by determining her transferable skills. One way I can describe this, is to tell the story of a woman who came to me for career counselling: Jane had been employed as a nursing supervisor, but found that with a young family, the shift work was seriously affecting her family. We concentrated on determining her transferable skills that could be used in many occupations.

There were:

a)  Supervisory experience;
b)  Interpersonal skills (cranky patients, their families, her staff. doctors, technicians etc.);
c)  Attention to detail (proper dosages of medication, concise medical records);
d)  Scheduling (making sure patients are prepared for surgery, getting them to X-ray and having medications on time etc.); and
e)  Many other skills and abilities.

When asked what she'd like to do as an alternative, she replied, *'I'd like to work with ladies' fashions, but know that I can never earn enough as a sales clerk.'*

I convinced her that she already had many of the skills that she would require, to *manage* a ladies' fashion store - she simply needed retail management courses to be able to switch her transferable skills into another completely different environment: In the retail industry she could use her existing skills:

   a) Supervisory experience; (supervise staff)
   b) Interpersonal skills (cranky customers, her staff, merchandisers, purchasing agents, delivery staff, etc.);
   c) Scheduling (ordering fashions – often eight or nine months ahead); and
   d) Pricing of items to remain competitive.

She went ahead and received training, and not only does she manage one dress shop, but is regional manager of a chain of ladies' dress shops!

You might suggest to your sister that she go to my web page and take career counselling on-line. She would go to:

www.dealingwithdifficultpeople.info/unique-career-counselling-service
that can help her identify twenty to forty occupations she could try.

A while back, I had to diversify the service my company offers to clients. My company offers training and development seminars world-wide. When I saw that company training budgets were being severely cut, I realised that I'd have to diversify for a while and use my other skills to take up the slack. Because my background is in human resources, I decided to offer my services to companies that were too small to have their own Human Resources departments. In addition (because I'm an author) I decided to try my hand at writing newspaper and magazine columns. All these activities allowed me to continue and thrive in a tight economy.

Your sister should start by writing down her transferable skills. A friend might help her do this because she may not identify all her talents and abilities herself. Then she would contact a career counsellor to help identify which occupations would utilise those transferable skills. She'll be surprised at the number of occupations that can utilise her existing talents and abilities. She may simply have to *"top up"* her knowledge by taking courses

What keeps us from making the necessary changes in our lives to better our existence? Most people resist change - it's easier and safer to do things the old way. In these hard, economic times, those who resist or fight change, take the chance that they'll be left behind. Others wait for others to force changes upon them - they react, rather than plan their own futures.

The cure for this often rests with the person's self-concept about his or her own capabilities. Many have not tested themselves to see whether they can do new tasks - it's simply too risky. They fear they may fail.

### *Only those who don't try - fail.*

### *Those who do try, but don't succeed - do exactly that - they don't succeed – but they haven't failed.*

## Destructive Child

*'My daughter has two children. The youngest is five. He can be a very sweet boy, but he's terribly destructive. Yesterday, his mother caught him setting fire to some paper in the bathroom sink. Another time, he got hold of a knife and cut the lounge suite. He throws his toys and once banged his door so hard the doorknob went into the wall. My daughter is so frustrated with him she doesn't know what to do.'*

Start by making sure that he is seen by a paediatrician who might also suggest he have a psychiatric or psychological evaluation. There could be a medical reason for his destructiveness and his behaviour could be related to his diet. She needs to have him assessed now, before he starts to school because the school will not tolerate that kind of behaviour. I wish her luck – because she's going to need it.

## Revenge!

*'My brother never forgets a slight and spends lots of time finding ways he can pay someone back for what they've done to him. He's always angry at someone or another.'*

He needs to stand back from his situation and analyse what's really happening when he's out for revenge. If he concentrates on getting revenge, it ties him to the wrongdoer, instead of allowing him to spend his energies on positive actions that will enrich his future. If he's able to deal with the issue right away - he should certainly do so but if he can't deal with the wrongdoer right away, he should drop the issue and not allow the thoughts of *"getting even"* to enter his mind. He'll find that *'What comes around - goes around'* and he'll just have to stand back and watch it happen. The offending person is usually punished in some way - without any intervention on his behalf.

He needs to remind himself, that if he's dwelling on the other person's negative acts, he's still giving the person control over his life. Is that person worthy of having this kind of impact on his life? I doubt it.

### Brother home from college

*'My brother has been away at college for four years. When he came back for school holidays, he always stayed in the guest room. Now he wants his old bedroom back (my room) and expects me to move into the guest room (which is much smaller). I don't think this is fair.*

*'He's also talking back to our Dad all the time and the tension in our home is very high for everyone involved. What can be done to get things back to normal?'*

Your parents are the ones who should decide who gets which bedroom, but I expect they will decide that you should keep the bedroom you've had. Your brother will not likely live at home for long once he obtains a job. He's at the stage where he's likely going to leave the nest soon anyway.

Your brother is not the same person who left for college. He's been off on his own making decisions and your parents had one less person to care for daily. Your parents may have enjoyed his absence. When a family finds themselves together again, the old rules and ways of relating often don't work. Students home from college may trigger old conflicts and introduce new ones. The way parents and their offspring relate during the student's coming and goings during school breaks can often give an idea of how things will be when the student returns home after his studies are completed.

To start, your parents need to arrange a family meeting to discuss expectations and be open to compromise. Parents need to identify important issues - getting a job, payment of rent, use of the car, household chores and participation in family activities. Household chores could include - no dirty dishes left in the sink or wet towels on the bathroom floor, responsible for his bedroom and bathroom. If your brother didn't want to comply with family rules and regulations he should be encouraged to move out.

## *Inter-racial Dating*

*'My brother is dating a Black girl and their relationship seems to be getting serious. My parents and I are really upset about this because we can look ahead to the time when they might marry and have children. I simply don't think I could accept their children. Imagine me being an aunt to a coloured baby?'*

Inter-racial, inter-cultural and inter-religious relationships are commonplace, although not always accepted, even by teens. But most of the time teens won't say so. They don't want to be perceived as racist. Parents, on the other hand, aren't always that discreet. Some harbour longstanding prejudices and loyalties and view their youngsters' dating behaviour as a betrayal.

Most of us think we've come a long way, but when it occurs in our own families - our own homes - it can be hard to accept. If the parents object - the couple may decide to continue dating, but behind their parent's backs. However, your brother needs to think long and hard about the consequences. He should contemplate how important his family relationship is to him. Will the trust of his family be lost to the extent that he won't gain it back? Is he sure this is the way he wants to exert his independence? Is he sure he wants to pay the price?

In many families, it's not all or nothing. Sometimes there's a middle ground. When parents raise children to be independent people they need to be prepared for them to be independent in ways they might not always understand. If they threaten to disown their child, they must consider the cost of exerting that kind of control. Are they willing to tear their family apart?

The family needs to start by having a family conference to discuss their concerns openly with each other. Both sides must confirm at the beginning of the discussion that they're there to listen to the other's side and that they'll keep an open mind. The discussion would include how you and your parents feel about the inter-racial relationship; your concerns about their future children; and society's attitude towards such relationships. His side would include why he has chosen this woman to be his partner. Only by discussing these matters openly, will the situation be resolved.

# CHAPTER 5

# DIFFICULT RELATIVES

How we interact with relatives has far more impact than the contact we may have with mere friends and co-workers. Unless we *"divorce"* ourselves from relatives, we need to learn coping mechanisms that keep the relationships healthy. Here are several situations you too may have faced in the past.

## *Competitive Nature*

*'My cousin, Jerry always wants to "beat me at something". His whole life revolves around being the best at everything. I don't have a competitive nature and find I'm uptight just being in the same room as he.'*

Let him know how you feel about his competitive approach to everything (using feedback):

**Describe his behaviour:**
*'Jerry you're always trying to get me to compete with you.'*

**How you felt when he acts that way:**
*'I get angry because you keep expecting me to compete with you.'*

**What you feel would be the solution:**

*'In the future, I'd like you to stop doing that and let me continue doing the best I can without feeling I have to compete with you.'*

You might add, *'As long as I try my best, I don't feel the need to compete with others.'*

If he continues his behaviour, use the feedback technique steps to deal with his repetitive negative behaviour, including a consequence should he act that way in the future. *'If you continue to insist on competing with me, I'll simply have to spend less time with you.'*

## *The Silent Treatment*

*'My Aunt Betty uses the "silent treatment" to get her way with my uncle. If she's upset about something, she clams up and refuses to talk to him. This can go on for days. My uncle has asked me to intervene and make her see how her behaviour is pushing him away from her. I want to help*

*save their marriage. What should I say to her that will change her behaviour?'*

This is a form of indirect aggression. Ignoring others, sulking or giving them the silent treatment by refusing to discuss issues with them, is manipulative and unfair to the recipient. This negative reaction is a no-win situation for both parties. Often the person giving the silent treatment wins the battle - but prolongs the war. If they don't settle issues (and remove the *"blips"* that have accumulated on their screen of annoyance) the issues will resurface later.

Let Aunt Betty know that this is *"dirty pool"* and an act of indirect aggression. Explain that they should discuss and resolve annoying situations immediately, so they don't accumulate and end up causing major blow-ups.

When I discuss the silent treatment at my seminars, I ask for input from my participants on whether they believe men or women use the silent treatment more. The consensus is that women use it far more than men. The explanations are that traditionally, women were not supposed to argue, so they gained the upper hand by refusing to talk about an issue. Later, when women felt more comfortable expressing their opposing opinions, they found they were still using this tactic. When asked why they were doing this, their reply was often, *'He never listens to me, so why should I bother expressing my opinion!'*

*'He never listens to me!'* comes from the differences in male-female communication styles. Because he's staring off into space, instead of giving eye contact and looking at her, making listening noises and nodding his head - she assumes he's not listening. This is often <u>not</u> the case. Explain this to Aunt Betty.

*'My uncle is the one who sulks and withdraws.'*

This doesn't mean that men don't use the silent treatment. On the contrary, almost 45 per cent of the silent treatment occurs when men refuse to talk about what's really going on inside themselves. This is likely because their problems usually involve the need to explain feelings, which most won't share with others.

For example, his wife notices that he's uncommunicative - usually a sign that something's wrong. She says, *'What's the matter, dear?'*

*'Nothing.'* he replies.

*'I can see there is. Won't you let me in on what's happening?'*

*'I told you, I don't want to talk about it!'*

This just puts the man on a bigger island of aloneness. Not only has he refused the well-intentioned help offered to him, but he's compounded the problem by pushing his wife away from him.

### Lateness

*'I often take my cousin-in-law Joanne, to community club meetings and shopping excursions but she's never ready when I come to pick her up! What can I do to solve this situation?'*

There are three basic kinds of time users. For instance, if they need to be at a 2:00 pm appointment:

a) Person comes in the door right at 2:00 pm.
b) Person comes in at 1:45 pm (or earlier – and gives the impression that he or she just made it!)
c) Person comes in at 2:10 pm (and acts as if he or she's on time - gives no explanation for his or her lateness).

People who fit (a) category often cut a fine line and occasionally fit into the (c) category.

People who fit (b) are on time, but some come too early and waste their valuable time waiting. If they're driven by the necessity to be early for everything, they should bring something to do during their waiting time.

People who fit (c) category (like your cousin) usually don't comprehend why others are so hostile towards them or why those who are waiting are upset by their tardiness. These people are late for events they don't want to attend, or they aren't ready when others expect them to be. They disrupt meetings, social events, concerts and lack consideration for other people's valuable time. By their actions (being late) they've shown those who are waiting, that *their* time isn't important (but their own is) therefore it's all right for others to wait for them. As everyone has only 168 hours every week to live, the people waiting object to others wasting their valuable time.

Tell her how you feel when she's late (using feedback) and explain that you're counting on her to be ready. Then, explain the consequences - if she isn't ready when you come for her, you'll simply leave without her. Then, do it!

## Partnership

*'My uncle wants me to become his partner in a small venture. It would not involve all my time, but I'm leery about starting **any** business partnership. I've seen too many of my friends become enemies after they became partners. How do I explain to him how I feel about this?'*

Going into a partnership, with a family member, relative or any another person is like getting married. Because of this, ask yourself the question, *'If my marriage was in trouble, where would I go for help?'* You'd likely go for marriage counselling. The same holds true if you're contemplating beginning a partnership or if a partnership's in trouble - the partners should get counselling - business counselling.

Remember too, that getting **out** of a partnership is as distressing as getting a divorce. Unless both partners work equally hard to make it work, the company's likely to fail. Be honest in explaining your concerns to your uncle. Talk the issues out. If there are more negatives than positives, tell him your family status and his friendship are too important to take the chance of entering a partnership with him.

## Needs Approval

*'I have to watch what I say to my cousin Brenda. She and I had the same level of position many years ago, but for some reason I've climbed the corporate ladder and she's had limited success. I've been reluctant to keep her informed about my successes because she's so sensitive about her own status. She feels that I'm too "taken up with my own importance to talk to her any more".*

*'Not only is she my cousin, but a former friend and I find I'm drifting away from her because of her attitude. How can I resolve this situation?'*

Brenda appears to have a low self-esteem level that may account for her inability to climb her own corporate ladder. Impress on her that you cherish her friendship and how you feel it's being undermined. Encourage her to take an assertiveness training course and praise her for her own successes. Explain to her exactly how you feel about not being able to share your successes with her.

## Destructive Grandchildren

*'I live with my son, his wife and three children. This became necessary when I broke my hip last year. I'm doing much better now, and I've*

*contemplated trying it on my own again. My present problem is trying to deal with my undisciplined grandchildren. They come into my bedroom without knocking and when I'm not there, they ransack my room. They've broken several of my belongings, but don't seem to show any remorse.*

*'Last night at dinner, I decided to say something about it. I bawled them out about their destructiveness and forbade them to come into my room unless I invited them. My daughter-in-law has been very cool to me since then. Was I wrong, to protect my belongings and expect the children to respect others' possessions?'*

I don't blame you for guarding your possessions. I've felt the same way myself when parents bring unruly children into my home. If children spill their milk or break something accidentally, I'm the first to forgive them. But if it's wilful or careless behaviour, I speak up. Your grandchildren needed guidance and their parents didn't seem to be providing it – you had every right to chastise them. However, you might have explained the problem to your daughter-in-law and asked her to speak to the children, rather than doing it yourself. Then if it happened again, you would speak to them yourself.

Start by speaking to your daughter-in-law. Tell her exactly what happened. Stick to the facts and tell her what they broke, when and how. Then ask her what she thinks would be a solution to the children's disregard to the importance of respecting others' possessions.

You also might ask yourself if her coolness might not be a result of accumulated agitation because of other difficulties in your relationship with her. Have you tried to help enough? Or have you helped too much (interfering with her *"space"?*) There could be underlying problems here and the only way to bring them to the surface is through open discussion.

If the tension doesn't lessen, then talk to your son and get him involved in trying to solve the problem. You also mention that you're contemplating trying it on your own. You may have to seriously look at this alternative if the situation doesn't improve.

### Office Romance

*'My cousin is having an office romance with her boss. I've warned her that this is going to end in disaster for her. She thinks nobody will*

*notice and that should her relationship break up – she and her boss will be able to handle it.'*

What causes or initiates most office romances? It happens simply because of proximity and availability. Married employees spend about the same length of time (and often more) with other gender co-workers - as they spend with their spouses!

It's amazing how fast co-workers catch on to the *"office romance"*. She may think she's pulled the wool over everyone's eyes, but her body language will probably give her away and there will be subtle differences in how she will interact with him. Most people believe that this kind of arrangement is fine and that it won't affect her chances of doing well with her company - but believe me it does. Others may assume that any promotion she receives was because of her personal relationship with her boss.

It can be uncomfortable for co-workers throughout the romance too, because they may perceive that she is a pipeline to upper management and will spill the beans about any mistakes they make. They also feel uncomfortable when the romance breaks up - and many don't know how to handle the situation. To be safe, she should stay clear of dating anyone she works with or has as a client. This would be especially deadly if she works in the middle or upper-management levels herself.

Occasionally office romances might work out - but the odds are that they won't. She needs to stop letting her hormones take over and instead concentrate on the consequences she'll have to face if the romance breaks up. When the romance sours and one of them decides to leave the company – often it's the woman, because she's likely in the more junior position. If neither employee goes - it will likely cause a serious strain on their office relationship.

### Ethnic Problem

*'I'm twenty-five years old. We have many family gatherings where I see my uncle. He's always making ethnic slurs and I'm tired of hearing them. What can I do other than leave the room when he starts this?'*

Jokes at the expense of someone else aren't jokes at all. Find a private time with your uncle where you could state, *'Uncle Charlie, I have something serious to say to you. You often offend me by using ethnic slurs and jokes and I don't find your comments the least bit funny.'*

Your uncle may insist that his comments are harmless. Your reply should be, *'Uncle Charlie, if they're harmless, then they're pointless, so I'd appreciate you keeping your prejudicial comments to yourself.'*

You may find Uncle Charlie isn't so friendly to you in the future, but he's likely to cut out the slurs at (least in your presence). If he continues with his slurs and ethnic jokes you might have to repeat your earlier comments (in public). As a last resort, you might let your family know that you want to limit the time you spend with him and tell them why.

## Car Death

*'My cousin James is inconsolable. His two-year-old daughter died because he had left her asleep in the back seat of his car on a hot day while he picked up a few groceries. When he returned, it took him several minutes before he realised that something was wrong with her. She had literally baked to death. He ran out of his car, screaming for help and a passer-by began administering CPR. The ambulance arrived within minutes, but it was too late.*

*'My problem is that I can't forgive him for what he's done. Time and time again we are warned that we just can't leave children or pets alone in a car on a warm or hot day! How can I ever forgive him?'*

It may take some time for you to do so. In the meantime, James will likely have to go through a court case to defend a manslaughter case - because he did kill his daughter. Both the law and society will make sure that he never forgets what he's done. It will take time, but I'm sure you will be able to handle this situation. You know that he did not do it on purpose and like everybody else - he makes mistakes - a very tragic one mind you - but a mistake.

## Gossip

*'My cousin, Georgina is a terrible gossip. I find that I end up telling her things then regret it soon after, especially if I learn that the matter has become common knowledge. How can I deal with her gossiping?'*

Gossip is another form of indirect aggression. It harms everyone involved. Tell your cousin that you will have to refrain from telling her anything of a personal nature and explain why. If you must tell someone, make sure that person will keep the confidential information to him or herself.

The person gossiping or talking behind the back of others doesn't allow the person to defend him or herself. For instance:

Margaret: *'Did you know that the police picked up Carmen's husband Patrick last night for drunk driving and he had to spend the night in jail?'*

How should you deal with or stop the gossip? Either ignore it or ask Margaret for facts. These facts would include names, dates, places, who started the information etc. Or you could suggest that you both go to the one the gossip is about (Carmen) and get her side of the story. Margaret will run for cover.

When gossip is passed from one person to another, it's inevitable that the meaning of the words changes somewhat. Here's the normal distortion of facts passed from one person to another over time:

### Distortion of Facts

      1st speaker: 100% correct
      2nd speaker: 60% correct
      3rd speaker: 40% correct
      4th speaker: 20% correct
      5th speaker: 10% correct

You'd be wise to check out rumours or gossip by going to the source of the information. Here's how Margaret's gossiping and perception of the situation were distorted as it was passed on:

Margaret: *'Did you know that the police picked up Carmen's husband Patrick last night for drunk driving and he had to spend the night in jail?'*

Diane: *'Isn't that the third time they've picked him up in the past year? I'll bet he has to stay in jail this time.'*

Margaret: *'I wouldn't be surprised if he did.'*

Margaret runs into another friend and states: *'Did you know the police picked Patrick up again last night for drunk driving and he'll probably have to spend a year in jail?'*

Brian: *'No, I didn't. I wonder why they'd make him stay in jail for a year?'*

Margaret: *'Well they've picked him up three times in the past year and that's the sentence he'll get.'*

Brian sees another friend and states, *'Patrick's in jail again because the police picked him up last night on a drunk driving charge. They're throwing the book at him and he'll be lucky to get his license back.'*

You can see how the facts got distorted in this case. There's no proof that:

a. Patrick **was** picked up for drunk driving.
b. That he received any sentence.
c. That they suspended his driver's license.

The truth was that Patrick had been going to Alcoholics Anonymous and had his drinking problem under control. The night before, he had stopped on the highway to help others who had been in a car accident. Someone had seen him talking with the police officer and had jumped to conclusions that the police had picked him up for drunk driving.

If you had been Diane and had heard the message (or any others in the chain of conversations) you should speak to those involved in the story.

You'd say, *'Carmen, there's a rumour going around that the police picked Patrick up for drunk driving last night. I felt you should know about it, so you can deal with it.'* You're not asking Carmen if it's true. It's up to her to confirm or deny the situation if she wants to.

### Stressed Brother

*'My brother started a new job in a hospital last month after being unemployed for six months. He's keen to do a good job. Unfortunately, he comes home from work so stressed, that he's shaking. What can he do to deal with the stresses he's under?'*

I'm sure you'll agree with me that in our modern society, stress is one of the most pressing problems (other than the economy of course, which, causes us stress). A prime candidate for high stress is an individual in a tension-filled work or home situation that feels powerless to cope with the stress or to change the conditions causing the stress.

Start by talking to him. Ask him what he thinks is causing him so much stress. People who work in the health-care field are top candidates for stress. He may be in the wrong kind of job for him. Carefully question him about his career choice to see if that is what's causing him so much stress. If that's not the problem, here are some steps he can take to relieve his stress:

- Physical exercise (must not be a competitive sport unless stress is caused by inactivity). Before beginning, he should check with his doctor.
- Listening to music or reading a good book.
- Getting away from it all by taking a nature walk, going fishing or playing a round of golf.
- Doing nothing (without feeling guilty because he isn't accomplishing anything).
- Joining a support group, meeting with friends and family.
- Organising his life. Disorganised people waste too much of their valuable time searching for lost articles. When time problems occur, his stress level will go up as well.
- Getting the proper amount of sleep and rest.
- TM (Transcendental Meditation) sets off a built-in mechanism that's the opposite of his fight or flight response.
- Biofeedback (only with a qualified health care technician).
- Having someone give a soothing massage can do wonders. If nobody's available, even a self-massage of stiff shoulders can help. He should check his stress levels several times during his working day. If he finds that his shoulders have tightened up again - he'd do some simple exercises to relieve the tension and/or self-massage to ease the tenseness.
- Allowing him solitude and private time at home if he seems to need it.
- Breathing deeply which sends needed oxygen to starved muscles, brain and vital organs.
- Laughing. Instead of watching a dreary movie or television program, encourage him to watch a comedy where he can laugh to relieve his tensions. Letting the *"little kid"* in him to have fun, is a pleasant way to get his feet back on the ground after a trying day.
- If he has stressors in other parts of his life or is committed to activities that are also draining his energies - suggest he drop some of them until his tension at work is lessened. If he's a Scout Leader, he may have to curtail being one for a while. If he has too many home responsibilities – try to have someone take over his share until he's better able to handle his work-life pressures.

### Compulsive Behaviour

*'My cousin's wife suffers from obsessive-compulsive behaviour. She does actions over and over. Just washing the kitchen floor takes her all*

*day, because she sweeps it, vacuums it and washes it four times. Then she gets down on her hands and knees and checks it all out again. I don't understand why she does these things, but I really want to support this couple and spend social time with them. What should I know about this illness?'*

There's little you can do as a friend, except encourage her to get medical help and counselling and to accept her as she is in the meantime. Her rituals are compulsions, because she needs order and symmetry in everything she sees and does. One book that can help you understand this disorder is **The Boy Who Couldn't Stop Washing** by Dr. Judith Rapoport.

### Agree to Disagree

*'The other day, my cousin and I were discussing the issue of abortion and we ended up in a shouting match and haven't spoken to each other since. How should I have handled this situation?'*

There are many topics that fit into this group, where you're on one side of an issue and a spouse, relative, friend or acquaintance is decidedly on the opposite. When you find yourself in this kind of conversation (where neither party will budge) say, *'You're entitled to your opinion, the same as I am. Let's agree to disagree and not talk about this topic in the future.'*

If the person continues to discuss the topic, state, *'I'm firm in my decision that we should drop this topic because neither of us is willing to compromise our opinions. Let's not talk about this any more.'*

If the person persists, use the stuck record technique, *'I've told you, I won't discuss this topic again.'* If necessary, ask them to account for their actions. *'Can you tell me why you brought up that issue again, when I've told you twice that I don't want to discuss this issue?'*

Make sure you use this technique only for exceptional situations, not as an excuse for situations where you simply want to win. Use it specifically for issues about values and morality.

### Whiners, complainers and bellyachers

*'My aunt is a negative-thinking person who is constantly complaining about something. I get tired of hearing her beefs, but because she's a relative, I must see her quite regularly. How can I get her to see how she affects people around her?'*

I too have had to deal with a negative-thinking person. She was always complaining about something, yet she had many good qualities that made me want to keep her as a friend. Because of this, I felt she warranted some help in overcoming her negative thinking.

One day when I had listened to three or four complaints (the same ones I'd heard voiced many times before) I decided to try to help her solve her problems. She was wasting so much of her energy just worrying about her problems that she had none left to spend on solving them. These are the steps I used with her and are the steps you could try with your aunt:

1. Get her permission to let you help her find solutions to her problems. *'I've heard you talking about these problems several times and you don't seem to have found solutions for them. Do you want me to see what I can do to help you solve these problems?'* If she refuses to let you help her solve her problems, say. *'If you won't let me help you, I don't want to hear about this problem again.'* If she agrees to let you help her:

2. Have her write down the problem including all necessary details. Make a separate list for each problem (there will probably be several). Deal with only one problem at a time.

3. Have her write down all the possible solutions to the problem. At this point *you* can suggest additional solutions.

4. Write down the pros (benefits) and cons (disadvantages) under each solution. Encourage her to be unemotional. Have her pretend the situation is happening to someone else and she's helping them determine the benefits and disadvantages of each solution.

5. Have her pick the best solution. This is the stage where she'll likely ask you, *'What do you think I should do?'* If you *do* suggest a solution and it doesn't work, she'll probably say, *'I told you it wouldn't work!'* (This type of person loves to pass the buck to someone else for his or her problems.) So, *she* must choose the best solution - not you!

6. Help her set some concrete goals that will make the solution happen. Include deadlines for their completion. This will keep her from procrastinating. After step 6, she's on her own. If she complains to you again about the problem:

7. Say, *'Why are we discussing this again? You know exactly what you need to do to solve this problem and you've chosen to do nothing about it. I don't want to hear another word about this situation except to hear that you've resolved the problem.'*

This process stops whiners and complainers from going on and on about the same problem. It also forces them to solve their problems - not just complain about them. If you find yourself complaining too much, try this process yourself. It will help you have a more positive attitude towards your ability to handle life's problems.

### Invades Privacy

*'My cousin Maryanne is a very nosy person. She worms private information out of me that I don't want her to have. I'm so mad at myself afterwards because she makes me reveal information that was given to me in confidence by a third person or private information about myself I don't want her to know. How can I stop her from coercing information out of me?'*

Understand that she didn't make you reveal the information. You decided to give it to her! Before you meet with her next time, decide what you will and will not talk about. When she brings up confidential matters you don't want to discuss, explain, *'I'd rather not discuss this with you.'* If she persists - use the stuck record technique until she realises that you won't budge.

You might ask yourself why you feel the need to break a confidence. Is it because you have so little else to talk about? Get more involved in things yourself and you won't feel the need to talk about what other people do or do not do.

### Intimacy

*'My cousin Rory phoned me the other day and said he needs me to help him with a problem he's facing with his wife. She hardly talks to him any more. She's mad at him because he won't talk about what's "inside" him - that he keeps too much to himself and won't share his feelings with her. She tells him she wants more intimacy, but he doesn't understand exactly what she wants from him. How can I help him with this problem?'*

When we look at relationships that survive, we see couples that are good friends and treat each other with respect. They have shared values and trust one another. Trust is the foundation of the relationship and without it - couples don't feel safe. If they don't feel safe, they can't be vulnerable. If they're not vulnerable, they can't be intimate.

Intimacy involves having complete trust in another person. He can obtain intimacy by *"letting it all hang out"* and allowing his wife to know what's happening inside him. This involves revealing how he really feels about what she does and considers her feelings when communicating with her. This involves a considerable amount of empathy. By revealing his true self, his wife can almost know how he'll react to situations and will try to stay clear of those that *will* upset him and find ways around difficult situations, so he won't feel hurt. He would do the same for her.

If you observe people getting to know each other (of the same or mixed genders) there are several steps, they take that allows them to get to the stage where they reach intimacy.

One person reveals trusting information. The second person accepts that trust and reveals similar information.

As the trust grows between these people, they enlarge their trust and reveal more and more.

This seems to be short-circuited in your cousin's relationship. His wife may be revealing information, but he's not reciprocating - therefore the intimacy can't advance further. In marriage, women use talk to create intimacy, where they openly express their feelings and thoughts. Men use touch to create intimacy (use non-verbal communication) and use talk to maintain independence. They're on guard to protect themselves from put-downs from others who might want to push them around. If they give others (even their wives) the weaponry (talk about their weaknesses) it could be used against them in the future. So, they clam up and resist verbal intimacy.

Most women are comfortable admitting negative feelings, but society has almost forbidden men to admit to weaknesses. Therefore, this limits their options for expressing their feelings. Society says they're allowed to show happiness and anger but are not allowed to show any feelings between those two emotions. Therefore, when men feel anxious, disappointed, jealous, sad, hurt, rejected, stupid, intimidated, insecure, ashamed or ignored – their outward appearance can show misleading verbal and non-verbal signs of anger. This ambiguous behaviour confuses women and adds to the male/female communication gap.

Many women complain that the men in their lives don't share their thoughts and feelings with them. They feel that their men don't trust them, so shut them out from learning what their feelings really are. This male vulnerability keeps many men and women from sharing true intimacy. Explain all this to your cousin and encourage him to be more forthright with his wife.

Some men take the chance and confide their innermost feelings to their wives. Unfortunately, their wives don't keep that information to themselves, so the men lose trust in their wives. Women should be very careful not to reveal their husband's confidential admissions about their feelings to others. If this has happened to Rory - he should discuss his feelings of betrayal with his wife.

### Uninvited Pets

*'Recently, my cousin and his family drove all day to stay with my family. They arrived with their two cats without asking in advance if it was acceptable. My family have animals, but we don't keep them in the house. We offered to put them in the garage, but they were horrified by the suggestion and were hurt that we suggested it. Did we handle this correctly?'*

It's extremely presumptuous to ever bring pets without asking if they will be welcome. You had the right to insist that they stay where it's convenient to you - not to them.

### Dysfunctional Upbringing

*'My cousin Jason grew up in a dysfunctional environment. He was beaten and yelled at most of his life and suffered from a barrage of constant put-downs. Repeatedly, he heard that he was "stupid, dumb and wouldn't amount to anything". He firmly believes that his future won't be any different from his past, so resists making decisions that will alter his life. How can I make him see that his future is what he makes of it and his past is not a blueprint for his life hereafter?'*

Many people spend their lives reliving the past. They get into a mental rut that concentrates on what was, rather than what will be. Many of their comments start with the prefaces, *'I should have...'* Or, *'If only I could...'* When people drift through life, rather than control it, I think of them as *"stuck"*. They'll remain stuck where they are unless *they* do something to change their lives.

They waste their lives by getting in a rut and stay there or at best make feeble stabs at changing their lives. The least kind of opposition sends them scuttling back towards their safety net of sameness. These people hate getting up in the morning, because there's not much that's exciting or stimulating in their lives. One day is just like another and the future's likely to be the same. These people need a jolt to get them living again. Just as heart attack victims need a jolt of electricity to get their hearts re-started, these people need a jolt of reality to put them back into the land of the living.

Let's put ourselves into Jason's shoes for a while and feel what he might be feeling:

He accepts criticism as always being true. Not only does he accept criticism from others willingly, he's the one who criticizes everything he does himself as well. The little voice in his head is always ridiculing him about his perceived failures. He punishes himself with statements such as *'I should have known that was going to happen. Where were my brains?'* He may state, *'I'm too old... Not smart enough... Am not good at that.'* What he's saying is, *'I'm a finished product in this area and I'm never going to be different.'*

His fear of failure is very often the fear of someone else's disapproval or ridicule. Failure is someone else's opinion of how certain acts should be completed, so he doesn't attempt anything new or challenging. He'll shun experiences that might bring failure and avoids anything that doesn't guarantee success. He may turn down excellent opportunities but can't explain why he's doing so.

He hasn't learned how to be assertive - to stand up for himself. Inexperienced in the art of getting his own needs met; he allows others to manipulate him. He's unable to make decisions that support his own wishes, values and feelings. The result is he feels bad about himself without knowing why.

He constantly compares himself to others. Others are always happier, more famous, more successful or worth more. Others' successes only make him more depressed at his own status in life. He may feel that if he fails at something, that he's a failure as a person. Instead of trying another avenue or another way of doing something - he quits trying.

Using 20/20 hindsight, he can probably see exactly where he went wrong – on a job interview or in a love relationship. These thoughts can cause immobility and make him remain in the negative rut he's in. Encourage him to stop thinking of life in black or white terms. There are many grey areas in between.

Deal with him by having a heart-to-heart with him. Identify his negative behaviour and ask his permission to bring this behaviour to his attention if you hear him running himself down or reliving his past.

If life doesn't come up to his expectations, console him with the idea that it's never too late for conditions to change. Instead of dwelling on the past, he needs to concentrate his energy on building a better, happier life and make the most of the present moment.

He can't acquire the trait of extending himself to the utmost overnight. Confidence is a cumulative feeling. There will likely be setbacks and disappointments, but remind him:

> *Someone who tries to do something and fails is a lot better off than the person who tries to do nothing and succeeds.*

Encourage Jason to get professional counselling to counteract his dysfunctional childhood and introduce him to good role models. Your moral support will make this transition considerably easier for him.

### Teen Abuse

*'My cousin Victoria and I (both only children) are very close – like brother and sister. We confide in each other and share our good and bad days. She came to me in tears explaining that her boyfriend had physically abused her. How could I have helped her? The only solution I could see to her problem was to confront her boyfriend and tell him to leave her alone.'*

Here's advice from a teen abuse clinic:

**If you are abused:**

Ways to make yourself safer if you are abused:

- Call the police if you have been assaulted.
- Tell someone. Talk to a parent, teacher, doctor, relative or counsellor. Have them keep a record for future evidence.
- Write down the details of the assault as soon as possible.
- Consider ending the relationship. Without intervention, his violence will increase in frequency and severity as time passes.
- Develop a safety plan. Know all the exits of your residence, memorise emergency numbers and know where you can stay in an emergency.
- Recognise that no one has the right to control you and that it's everyone's right to live without fear.

### Early warning signs of teen dating violence:

Are you going out with someone who?

- Is jealous and possessive towards you, makes you choose between him and friends and relatives, checks up on you and won't accept breaking up?
- Tries to control you, gives orders, makes all the decisions and doesn't take your opinion seriously?
- Criticizes the way you dress, talk and dance?
- Is scary or threatens you? Do you worry about how the person will react to things you say or do?
- Do you "walk on eggs" when you're around him?
- Is he violent? Has a history of fighting, losing his temper quickly, bragging about mistreating others?
- Pressures you for sex? Is forceful or scary about sex, thinks women or girls are sex objects and attempts to manipulate you?
- Abuses drugs or alcohol and pressures you to take them?
- Blames you when you've been mistreated?
- Believes men should be in control and powerful and women should be passive and submissive?
- Your family and friends have warned you about the person?

### If *you* are abusive:

- You need to take responsibility for your behaviour; your girlfriend does not make you hurt her.
- Your violence will increase, if you don't act to stop it.
- Blaming your violence on drugs, alcohol or sickness and apologising after the violence will not solve the problem.
- Physical violence and threats of violence are crimes. You face fines or imprisonment if convicted.
- You can begin to change the way you act with the support of local counselling agencies.
- Let her know you're seeking help and support her if she decides to report the incident(s) to the police and follow-through with the steps described.

*'My wife was abused as a child and I almost feel as if a spirit is in our bedroom with us. She cringes at my touch and I know she hates anything related to sexual relations. Colleen's stepfather had abused her giving her memories of uncomfortable things he did to her and the twisted games he did to punish her. Her abuse started at age six and continued until she was eleven. The sexual abuse stopped but psychological abuse took over. He would do things like shutting off the*

*hot water when she was having a shower. He acted like a jealous boyfriend. Her mother was aware of what was happening but didn't step in to stop him. How can I help her?'*

Professional help is an absolute must for your wife. Be there and support her through the difficult steps she will face. Sexual abuse is such an isolating act that it makes the victim feel secluded and alone in her pain. An ally can help remove that feeling. Start by buying her a book entitled, ***What about me? Stop Selfishness from ruining your relationship*** by Dr. Jane Greer. It is the story about a woman who suffered from a similar situation and describes her husband's frustration when he didn't know what to do to help her.

Part of her recovery was to dredge up awful memories and feelings, which took tremendous patience on the part of her husband. The survivor of abuse needs to feel empowered with the ability to say *'No'* to sex. It's something they weren't allowed or able to do, when they were children. Not only will she have to deal with the sexual abuse by her step-father but will need to forgive her mother for standing by and allowing it to continue.

### Adult Abuse

Janice and Tony had a big argument three months after their marriage, and she refused to have sex with him that night. The next morning the air was frigid. They were to have dinner at his parent's place that night and because he had promised his father he would help him dig his garden, they'd left their home shortly after having their lunch. As soon as they arrived at his parents' place, Tony went into the back yard to help his father. Janice was left with his mother, Nellie. Nellie was rather a chatterbox and with Janice's raging headache she didn't want to be rude to her mother-in-law. She loved the woman but couldn't tolerate her constant chatter – not today anyway.

*'I promised a friend that I would stop in and see her this afternoon. Seeing Tony will be busy this afternoon, it will be a good time for me to go see her.'*

Janice got in their car and drove to Adele's home that wasn't far from her in-law's place. She wasn't home, so Janice went to a fast food place and had a cup of tea. She returned to her in-laws home less than an hour after she'd left. As she drove into the yard, she saw that everyone was gathered around the back door of the home. Tony's dad, Frank strode over as Janice was exiting the car.

115

*'What are you doing driving Tony's car without his permission?'* he shouted.

*'Just what I need.'* she thought. She'd just calmed herself down but was instantly angry again. How dare this old man tell her what to do!

*'This is now my car as well as Tony's and I have every right to drive it whenever I want to.'* she tried to say calmly.

*'Tony bought it, so he owns it.'* was Frank's retort.

*'So, I suppose he should ask my permission every time he sleeps in the bed I bought or eats at the kitchen table or sits on the sofa I bought?'* she roared back.

Tony suddenly stepped between them. He was still furious at Janice for the argument they'd had the night before, *'Don't you dare talk to my father that way!'* he shouted at Janice as he lifted her bodily from the ground.

His fingers gripped her upper arms so tightly she couldn't move. He carried her this way for fifty feet until he reached the public sidewalk at the front of his parent's home. He placed Janice's feet roughly on the ground, turned her around and kicked her in the buttocks with his work boots. *'Get out and stay out!'* he bellowed.

No one in his family had attempted to intervene between them. Janice thought that at least Tony's brother Jason would have stepped in to help her. She staggered a few steps then regained her balance and kept walking away from Tony – tears streaming down her face. Her purse was still in the car, so she had no money. What was she going to do? Where was she going to go? She just knew she couldn't go back to his parent's home. When she got to the corner of the street, she peered back to see whether anyone had followed her. No one had.

Her own parents lived about ten blocks away, so she started walking towards their home. She noticed that Tony's fingernails had pierced the backs of both her upper arms and they now had rivulets of blood running down them. As she passed a petrol station, she decided to ask whether she could use their washroom facilities to clean up her arms and use their phone to call her parents.

The elderly male attendant at the petrol station took one look at the distraught young woman and immediately thought *'Rape. This girl has been raped.'* and rushed over to assist her. She was as pale as a ghost and he led her to a chair behind the counter and brought her a glass of water. Everyone in the place was staring at her. The man asked a female customer to get some wet paper towels from the washroom, so he could clean up her arms. Then he went to the first aid kit in the staff room, applied a disinfectant and carefully dressed her wounds.

*'Thank you so much,'* murmured Janice. *'Would you please let me use your phone? I want to phone my parents.'*

*'Of course you can. Do you want me to call the police?'* he asked.

Janice gave the man a startled look then suddenly understood why he'd said what he did. *'No, that's not necessary. My parents will look after this.'*

Janice hadn't want anyone at the petrol station to know what had happened to her, so when her mother answered the phone she said, *'Mom I'm at Jackson's petrol station on Davidson Road. Can you please pick me up right away?'*

Diane could hear from Janice's voice that something was dreadfully wrong but didn't question her. *'I'll be right there.'*

Diane arrived in record time and was upset to see Janice in such a condition. *'What happened?'* she asked the attendant.

*'We don't really know. She just walked in here asking to use the washroom and phone. But she had blood running down both arms and looked as if she was going to pass out. I've cleaned the wounds and dressed them. I hope she'll be all right.'* replied the concerned attendant.

*'Well thank you for taking such good care of her,'* added Diane.

As soon as they were driving, Janice told her mother everything that had happened since the evening before and as soon as they arrived home Diane phoned Janice's father Jim at work. He worked only minutes away and came right home. Janice explained again what had happened. *'Do you want me to drive you home to get some of your clothes?'* he asked.

*'I don't have my purse, so don't have the keys to get in.'* she replied.

*'That's all right. Seeing we're your landlord, we have an extra set.'* Janice's parents had rented their investment property to the couple.

They quickly drove over to Janice's home, retrieved a suitcase from the garage that Janice filled with work, casual clothes and toiletries. She saw her father glancing at the torn pyjama bottoms that were still lying in their bedroom floor and shook his head. *'I'll make him pay if he ever hits or harms you again!'* he raged.

They left, and Janice returned to her parent's home. They put her things into her old bedroom and she slept well that night. The next morning, Janice returned to work, but made sure she wore a long-sleeved outfit, so her bandages would not be visible.

For six days, she didn't hear from Tony. Finally, that Saturday morning he phoned. Jim answered the phone when he called.

*'Can I speak to Janice please?'* Tony wanted to know.

*'I doubt if she wants to talk to you after what you did to her.'* was Jim's reply.

*'I want to apologise to her for my behaviour and ask her to come home.'* he said earnestly.

Jim turned away from the phone, *'Janice, do you want to talk to Tony?'*

First, she shook her head, but when her father told her what Tony had said, she agreed to speak with him.

Tony repeated his apologies and told her that such a thing would never happen again. *'Can I come over to see you?'*

Janice looked at Jim, *'He wants to come over to see me.'*

*'Just remind him that your mother and I will be here, and he'd better not start any trouble.'* he added worriedly.

Tony promised he wouldn't and arrived a short time later. Even though Jim was six inches shorter and many pounds lighter than he, Tony was intimidated by the man and almost turned back instead of ringing the bell. However, he built up his courage and rang the bell. Jim met him at the door and ushered him into the living room. Janice and her mother stayed in the kitchen. Jim stood before Tony and said plainly and clearly, *'If you ever harm my daughter again, so help me I'll make you wish you weren't alive!'*

Tony nodded his head, *'I promise I will never harm her again. Now can I talk privately with her?'*

*'Yes, but remember we'll be in the next room.'* was Jim's reply as he glared at Tony.

*'Okay.'* Tony said as he looked at the carpet.

Jim went to fetch Janice and she squared her shoulders before she left the kitchen. She was apprehensive about being in the same room with Tony, knowing the kind of a temper he'd revealed to her that past Sunday afternoon. But when she entered the room she saw that Tony was sitting on the sofa with his head in his hands sobbing. He looked up when she entered the room with such anguish on his face, that she couldn't remain furious with him.

He stood up and cautiously approached her, *'I'm so sorry I hurt you. I shouldn't have done what I did either Saturday night or Sunday. Did I hurt you very much?'* he asked as he started examining her.

She'd waited till that morning to take the bandages off her arms, but the marks and bruises still looked very sore and tender. *'Oh my God.'* he said as he looked at them. *'I can't believe I did that to you!'*

*'Well you did, and I need you to promise that you'll never do anything like that again.'* she admonished him.

*'I do. I do. Can you ever forgive me?'* he said contritely.

*'I'll forgive you this time, but I will walk out for good if you ever hurt me again.'* was Janice's emphatic reply.

Janice gathered her things, gave her parents a big hug and went home with Tony. Before she left, she told her parents that Tony was truly sorry and had promised that he would never harm her again. Jim just shook his head as he said, *'Time will tell. Time will tell.'*

At first Janice refused to go to Tony's parent's home for their usual Sunday noon meals, but after several weeks Tony begged her to go, so she relented. Janice and Frank were never destined to be close. Frank had refused to apologise for his outburst and Janice certainly wasn't going to give in to the tyrant. She had to steel herself before each visit, telling herself that she wouldn't argue with him. Frank and Janice seldom if ever spoke directly to each other and you could cut the air with the hostility between them. Nellie sat looking from one to the other shaking her head and was upset that their feud was not resolved.

Six months after their marriage, Janice realised that even though Tony did not physically hurt her, he did many things that were emotionally abusive. She left him and got on with her life.

119

### Destructive Child

*'My daughter has two children. The youngest is five. He can be a very sweet boy, but he's terribly destructive. Yesterday, his mother caught him setting fire to some paper in the bathroom sink. Another time, he got hold of a knife and cut the lounge suite. He throws his toys and once banged his door so hard the doorknob went into the wall. My daughter is so frustrated with him she doesn't know what to do.'*

Start by making sure that he is seen by a paediatrician who might also suggest he have a psychiatric or psychological evaluation. There could be a medical reason for his destructiveness or his behaviour could be related to his diet. She needs to have him assessed now, before he starts school because the school will not tolerate that kind of behaviour. I wish her luck – because she's going to need it.

### Out of control Teens

*'My sixteen-year-old nephew was thrown out of his home last week and I've agreed to take him in. His father has explained that he's been acting very aggressively lately. He shouts at his sister, his friends and is disrespectful of adults. He's also started throwing things around when he's mad. He's out of control. How can I deal with his disruptive behaviour and set some ground rules while he stays with us? My main goal is to get him home with his family again.'*

In many other animal species, the offspring are already on their own when they reach the age of reproduction. In humans, the age of reproduction is reached at puberty (11 to 14). Yet, the *"man-cubs"* live at home for another five to ten years. This results in a dilemma; near-adults being parented by fully-grown adults. Ironically, the teenager is usually taller and heavier than his mother and sometimes even his father. The stage is set for a potentially explosive situation.

Start by taking him to a doctor to eliminate medical reasons for the unacceptable behaviour. If his behaviour does not have a medical reason, both you and his parents should join a Toughlove group. In Australia, they can be found on www.toughlove.org.au.

This is a self-help group for parents troubled by their children's destructive and hurtful behaviour. At Toughlove groups, you will find acceptance and support and learn new successful ways of dealing with teen problems. Although Toughlove is not run by professionals, is not a therapy group and does not profess to work miracles, it can change your own behaviours and attitudes and find new strategies for dealing with problems. It's about finding toughness within yourselves. It's about children taking responsibility for their behaviour and suffering the consequences when they do something wrong.

Today it often seems that the children have all the rights. Toughlove groups advocate that parents have rights too. This organisation has helped many parents who have incorrigible teens. It is a support group for parents. These groups are not there to blame anyone, because at this point, it doesn't matter what caused the problem. The issue is - how to solve the situation. You will know that it's time to join such a group if your nephew has done the following:

**Your teenager has run away:**

- Overnight;
- For two days;
- For a week;
- For more than a week.

**Your teenager has:**

- Missed dinner;
- Been late;
- Been stoned or drunk;
- Didn't come home at all;
    - Overnight,
    - For two days.
    - For a week,
    - For more than a week.

**At Home:**

- You and your spouse argue about your teenager's behaviour.
- You have withdrawn from your spouse.
- Your spouse has withdrawn from you.
- You have not had a peaceful night's sleep.
- You hate to hear the phone ring when your teenager is not home.
- You or your spouse have lost time from work because of your teenager.

**At school, your teenager has been:**

- Tardy;
- Absent;

- Playing hooky;
- Suspended;
- You've been called by the school for bad behaviour.

## Your teenager has been violent:

- Verbally;
- Physically to the house or furniture;
- Physically to you, your spouse or your children;
- Physically to other people;
  - In school,
  - With the police.

## Legally, your teenager has:

- Received summons;
- Received fines;
- Received tickets;
- Been involved in accidents;
- Been charged with drug incidents;
- Been charged with drinking;
- Been arrested.

If there are two areas in the school category, two areas in the home category and one area in the legal category, the crisis is building. If you've checked more areas, the family is already in crisis and should contact your local Toughlove group for help. They can help when parents have tried everything else from police to social services and find traditional methods don't work.

Parents need to make a list of *"non-negotiable"* rules. Some of the standard ones could be no drinking and driving, no lying and no swearing in the home. Parents need to set a *"Bottom Line"* - something they want to accomplish with their teenager. It might be something as simple as insisting they take out the garbage, clean their room or use head phones when they play their music. Find your nearest Toughlove group and attend a meeting.

Do it now - your nephew's family's future depends on it.

### *Obesity*

*'My cousin Richard has a weight problem. He's tried about fifteen diets - one for every year of his life. He uses his weight as an excuse for not*

*participating in sports or going to school dances. He's constantly teased at school about his weight, feels uncomfortable in groups and is too embarrassed to participate in gym classes. How can I help him overcome his problem without nagging?'*

Many children try to follow their doctor-ordered diets but find themselves weak with hunger. Some revert to sudden uncontrollable eating and suffer from the guilt that inevitably follows. Richard is likely desperate to fit in with his peers and is likely anxious for someone to help him. Unfortunately, there are no quick fixes - he needs to do it for himself.

Most eating disorder programs focus on bulimic or anorexic females, which might discourage him from joining an eating disorder clinic. In terms of sheer numbers, there are far more obese children than bulimic or anorexics but eating disorder programs seem to concentrate most of their efforts on those two problems. This is likely because of the fear of impending death for those who starve themselves or continually purge food.

There are few regulated treatment programs for obese boys, unless they go to regular weight loss clinics. Occasionally summer camp programs for kids with eating disorders help, but few have follow-up programs to keep them on the path to healthy eating. Suggest that his parents investigate to see if there are special programs available to help him deal with his weight problem. Encourage them to be persistent until they find the right one for him.

Show your ongoing encouragement for his efforts and help him to accept himself for who he is. Make him understand that his self-esteem doesn't depend on his weight. He needs to learn how to form relationships that aren't based on his size.

If his excess weight is genetic, he'll need to establish at an early age, a lifetime habit of eating nourishing, low-fat foods. Overweight children often live with overweight parents. His parents need to set an example for him by eating a proper diet themselves. It will make it easier for him to follow that diet throughout his life, if he starts now. His daily activity requires exercising and he should be encouraged to limit his television viewing time.

Be sure to read the earlier information about obesity.

### *How to obtain the salary she's worth*

*'My cousin is always complaining that she isn't paid what she's worth. She's going to a job interview next week and is anxious to receive a proper salary. What kind of advice can I give her, so she'll obtain the salary she's worth?'*

Women who want equal pay for work of equal value must learn to stand up for themselves and negotiate the salaries they're worth, just as successful men do. And they must look at the full package deal - not just the salary. This includes extended holidays, a larger office and support staff. They should make sure their company pension-plan benefits are the same for women as men.

Companies normally offer a woman a lower salary than a man, so before she goes to an interview, she needs to do her homework and determine the salary range of the position she's applying for. She would obtain this information by phoning the company representative who's responsible for filling the vacancy. Some may be reluctant to give her the salary range. If they balk, she would say, *'I need to know the salary range, because I'm afraid I might be overqualified for the position.'* They'll usually give it to her if she states this.

Let's suppose your cousin hasn't learned the salary range before her interview. The recruiter asks her: *'What are your salary expectations?'* She's earning $25,000 in her present position, but she knows there are more responsibilities in the new position. So, she says that her salary expectations are $28,000. She feels she'll be happy with a $3,000 a year raise.

She's way off base in this case! If she had done her homework, she might have found that the salary range for this position (normally filled by a male) was $30,000 to $40,000. She goofed! Of course, they're going to hire her for $28,000! But she'll be grossly underpaid for what she'll be doing - from the start of her employment and thereafter.

Now let's assume she did her homework in advance and learned that the salary range was $30,000 - $40,000. What should she have told them her salary expectations were? Would she say $30,000 (as most women would)? Or $38,000 (as most men would)? So, she asks for $38,000. They're bound to negotiate with her and she'll probably settle on about $36,000 as her starting salary. That's $8,000 more per year or $666 more a month than the $28,000 she was originally willing to take! Quite a difference!

And it doesn't end here either. The woman who accepted the $28,000 starting salary would probably qualify for a cost-of-living increase after a year with the company. Let's say it's five percent. This would bring her salary up to $29,400. The second year's increase is the same, so her salary would go up to $30,870. If, however, she had obtained $36,000 originally - after a year she would be making $37,800 and after two years, $39,690. This would be $8,820 more! The gap is increasing between what she should have been getting and what she agreed to accept. And the gap will get larger and larger, unless she negotiates properly at the beginning of her employment.

If the recruiter asks what she was earning in her last position, she should explain that she was underpaid for the duties of her position, so it isn't relevant to the position she's applying for (unless it's close to the salary range they're offering).

Initially, she may find it difficult to negotiate this way, but she must feel she's worth it. Employers wouldn't assign salary ranges to these positions in the first place if they weren't worth that dollar amount.

*'My cousin has a clerical position and wonders how she can obtain a management position.'*

If she's not sure how to get a higher paying position, suggest that she:

1.  Go through the career counselling process (see Appendix A for a source) to decide what kind of occupation she wishes to pursue and determine how she would obtain it. Would it be reached through on-the-job training (not likely) or would she require formal education and/or training?
2.  Once she found out, she'd need to obtain that training (if necessary working at a junior level in the field of work she's chosen).
3.  She'd document every task she did in her present position and determine whether she was doing an important part of her supervisor's job. She'd look for those tasks that required independent action or decision-making on her part. She'd find that if she could point out that she made at least some decisions, she could convince her employer that she can make major ones too. She'd just be using different kinds of data. Then she'd look for duties where her judgement was crucial in the outcome of the task and look for clear-cut areas of responsibility, authority and accountability. In other words, she would look for things she did

on a regular basis where she decided the outcome. These are the skills management requires and they pay well for them.

4. She'd ask her boss if her talents could be utilised in other areas of her department and explain that she'd be willing to take a demotion in salary for this chance. (Even a junior position - one with a toehold on the bottom rung of the ladder - is better than a clerical or support position). If her boss doesn't think this is a good idea – she should speak to a Human Resources representative. She'd explain to him or her what decision-making qualities she's developed and what specialty she'd like to get into. S/he would be asked to keep her informed of any positions that came up that would suit her qualifications. As a back-up, she'd watch the company job bulletin board and apply for positions she thought she could handle.

5. If she decided to go outside the company, she'd stay clear of any advertisements that used the words to describe the position or the candidate: skills, right arm, high class, bright, achiever, hard working, support services, assistant to, pleasant working conditions. These denote low-level positions. She'd watch for those saying: self-starter, career oriented, challenging position, etc.

6. She would need to obtain her family's help at home, so she could concentrate more on her career.

### Know it all

*'My brother is a know-it-all and I have trouble dealing with him. He asks me for information, and then insists on giving me his version of what he believes is the answer.'*

First, listen to his ideas. Then ask him for facts relating to his information (statistics, figures, etc.). Then, using information available to you, tell him the facts. Refer to written data if necessary. Most *"know-it-alls"* can't back up their comments with hard facts and data.

### Share a vehicle

*'My sister and I share an additional car in our family. One of our rules is that nobody smokes in the car. However, often when it is my turn to use the car, I find it reeks of cigarette smoke. I don't want to rat on my brother by telling our parents, but I am allergic to cigarette smoke and find I must leave all the windows down every time I use the car. How*

*can I make him comply with this ruling? I think it is his friends that smoke – I doubt if it is him smoking.'*

This is another classic case where you can use feedback:

a) **The problem** *– He's allowing someone to smoke in the car.'*
b) **Your feelings or reactions** *– 'You know I'm allergic to cigarette smoke and you know you're breaking the rules.'*
c) **Solution** *– If you do that again, I'll have no choice but to tell Mom and Dad about it.'*

### Freezes under pressure

*'My single mother freezes whenever an emergency happens at home. She becomes immobilised - frozen to the spot. If she must make an important decision, she puts it off until others are forced to make those decisions for her. In group situations she becomes mute and seems unable to speak. What's happening here?'*

When her fight or flight response kicks in, instead of either fighting or running away from the danger, she simply freezes. She doesn't make decisions because she's afraid she'll make the wrong one. This again immobilises her. She becomes speechless because she seems to be highly prone to stage fright.

Her behaviour is very passive, so suggest that she take an assertiveness training course. Help her learn how to make decisions. When she's forced to decide, talk to her privately and ask her, *'What do you think you should do? Why did you make that decision? What other alternatives are open to you?'* If you're the one needing her to make the decision - give her deadlines and check with her along the way to see if she needs more information before making her decision.

These sound like well entrenched behaviours that may require professional help to overcome. She's likely had some horrific situations in her past that have caused her immobilisation.

# CHAPTER 6

# DIFFICULT SENIORS

## *How seniors deal with retirement*

Retirement can be a difficult transition for the seniors in your life. If you understand what happens during the transition, you can help them deal with the many changes they'll face.

Statistics now prove that men can retire earlier and with fewer cares than women can, because seventy per cent of men and only fifty-one per cent of women have pension plans. Working women don't plan to retire or retire as early as men do, unless they're married, and their husbands have a good income. This is because women traditionally enter the work force later than men and have built up less in their pension funds.

An emerging trend shows that when husbands retire, many of their wives decide to stay in the workforce. The women's reasons for doing so relate to money (or lack of it) continued family medical and pension benefits, their own job satisfaction and sense of identity. Their husbands may have been in the workforce for forty-five years, but many wives are five to fifteen years younger than their spouses and have only worked for twenty or twenty-five years. Many aren't ready to retire.

Women who marry older men or marry for a second time may still be in the middle of their career paths when their husbands retire. Many husbands object to the reversal of traditional roles where they're the homemakers and their wives are the breadwinners. This can affect the man's ego and power struggles can occur. Couples who are approaching this milestone in their lives should look carefully at the upheaval this might cause in their relationship. They need to take steps to lessen the perceived problems - before retirement!

Divorced women spend three more years in the work force than married or widowed women. This shows that women usually come out of a divorce worse off economically than men. Widows can collect from their husband's pension fund as well as from their own. Unfortunately, pension funds are not as kind to divorced women. They end up with only their own pension fund to count on, even though in their marriage, they may have stayed at home and cared for their children for many years. Many are exempt from receiving benefits from their ex-spouse's pension fund, but laws in many countries have been changed to stop this inequity.

Many retired people (especially those who equate their worth with how much they earn or how much work they do) may face a lowered level of self-esteem. They may miss having something to get up for, something that makes them feel productive. Encouraging them to keep active and productive can be the best advice we can give them.

### *Growing Old*

When you age, are you going to be an old matriarch, dressing in lace and leaving the comfort of the armchair only to say and do what's expected of an old lady? Are you going to be an old patriarch, shuffling in your slippers to and from the local store every day to get a newspaper? Or are you going to flaunt your grey hair, tell it like it is and live for the joy of the moment? One woman celebrated her sixtieth birthday by getting her ears pierced and her husband took flying lessons. Seniors can either celebrate their life accomplishments and live out their days with zest and joy or sink into despair about the missed opportunities and physical and social limitations of aging in a youth-oriented society.

Most of us have a picture of the old man who becomes more and more crotchety as the years go by who constantly criticizes his family members for being and living a different way. Often their happiness is bound up in others' actions. There are finally enough ours in a day to do all the things they've wanted to do, but don't seem to have the drive to do them. Unfortunately, so many have lived their adult lives being productive and find it extremely difficult to turn off that productivity. However, this doesn't mean that they can do without having something to get up for. If seniors don't have something to get up for - they soon shrivel up and wither away. Many die too young and it has nothing to do with their age – it relates to how old they feel they are.

Learning to redirect energy to new roles and activities keeps the mental and physical juices flowing. It allows seniors to focus on life's journey – not on the destination. Even small changes can add an exciting quality to life and keep them from living in the past by tasting a new food - riding a bus to a different destination - learning a new craft. They volunteer now that they have time - share experiences with friends - tell their grandchildren experiences they had as a child. Regardless of circumstances, it's possible to enjoy the journey until the end.

Free and happy seniors don't fit the social stereotype of the lonely and enfeebled old-timer. Many have survived world wars and depressions, are very capable people and we underestimate their abilities. Some are still taking courses at the university, hiking and swimming. They attend plays, concerts, go out for dinner and even love rock and roll. Others begin new things – like learning how to play the piano.

Karla is one of these seniors. She admits that being a nurse was a giving profession, but she got very little in return. Now that she's retired, she describes herself as a loner and needs lots of time for herself. Karla is typical of a growing number of older people who guard their privacy, independence and freedom like Rottweilers. They live alone - and love it. Well-meaning children and grandchildren are concerned - but have little need to be. She wouldn't want to be all mixed up living amongst family. She values her independence and privacy too much. She also believes that her children have a right to live on their own, without a parent hovering over them.

Here are the essential ingredients for a happy, solo senior:

**Health** - They don't have to have the body of a seventy-year-old Swede - just enough physical fortitude to get through the day alone or with a helping hand from homemakers, housecleaners or helpful family members.

**Money** - The great leveller. If they have money, they can live anywhere and anyhow they want.

**Affordable Housing** - Now in short supply. This is the top expense and top concern for seniors, especially older, single women who make up the second largest segment of the population living in poverty. Housing must be near amenities and resources, so they don't have to take a taxi to the grocery store. Economics may force them to move in with sons or daughters.

**Social Support** - Most countries have an impressive array of social services for seniors. Resources such as Meals on Wheels and other homecare services make later life easier.

**Emotional Support** - It doesn't really matter who it is - a family member, an old friend or an empathetic neighbour. Someone's got to care whether s/he gets out of bed every day.

**Community Involvement** - Those who thrive are those who belong to an active community of peers - a church, a seniors' club or a housing community. It isn't how often they see their children - it's how many places in the world they are somebody.

**Hobbies and Intellectual Pursuits** – Shuffle-board? Bingo? Lawn bowling? Ceramics? Not quite. Community involvement and volunteerism, university or fitness courses, travel, writing and entertaining are among the most common pastimes of active seniors.

*Memory*

A senior makes a phone call and when the person answers the call, they state, *'I'm sorry - I've forgotten who I'm calling. Can you tell me the company name please?'* Scenes like this are becoming common as people enter their senior years. Yet another pair of eyeglasses goes astray. More and more *"belated birthday"* greetings get sent. Important pieces of paper – some, in fact, lists of things not to forget – sit gathering dust in special places that have somehow escaped their memory. With them go the names of those we met yesterday and of people we've known since our hair was its original colour.

Most people will experience memory loss and if we can do something about it we should. In an age when Alzheimer's disease gets so much publicity, anxiety about memory loss is very common. Whether or not they agree with the inevitability of memory loss with age, experts say there are ways to develop a person's recall.

Here are some things to try:

- When you meet a person, be sure to repeat their name as often as three times.
- Ninety per cent of memory function is visual. People who are visual are ahead of the game. Here's one way to exercise your visual memory. Choose a detailed photo from a magazine and examine it closely for 30 seconds. Then cover the picture and list everything in it you can remember. After a few trials with different pictures, chances are your visual recall will improve.
- Stimulate your imagination. Television is one of the biggest enemies of memory. Reading a book gives you words and you need to imagine pictures to go with it. By giving you both pictures and words, television takes away that imaginative factor.
- If you can't remember something you want to - try not to feel guilty. The sooner your anxiety level drops, the sooner memories will come back.

## *Early Retirement*

*'I never dreamed that my job was in jeopardy. During my five years as office manager, I heard nothing but compliments about my work. Last week, however, I was let go. My boss said sales had dropped so low that he couldn't afford my salary. I keep wondering why I didn't see it coming. I'm fifty-two years old - who's going to hire me at my age? I've lost more than my paycheque - I've lost faith that hard work pays off and I've lost part of my identity.'*

Wendy felt numb and went through the stage of, *'This can't be happening to me!'* Then she felt panic - pictured her home being up for sale and finding herself destitute. Then she felt angry. *'After all my hard work – unemployment is a cruel reward.'* As she passed along the grieving process, she next felt depressed. *'Why bother sending out more resumes? Nobody's going to respond.'* Finally came acceptance where she gradually came to terms with what had happened. She sat down and seriously went over her finances and realised that she had her husband's pension and her home was paid off. If she worked only part-time she would be able to manage until she could take an early retirement and could live on her own pension funds. Things weren't as bad as she thought and if she belt-tightened a bit, she'd be able to manage.

Some companies are offering severance packages to people in their mid-fifties. If people have planned for retirement and the packages are good - there's no problem. However, if the packages are small and they haven't prepared, can't get a job elsewhere or don't have enough money to do the things they like - it can be very difficult for the individual.

Some early retirement programs produce negative emotions that could lead to an increase in suicide. Severance packages can lead to loss of employment, income security and prestige in the community or business world. When we see a series of losses piling up on a person - we see an increase in suicide. Society brings that on a lot earlier if it takes people out of the employment field and say, *'You're no good any more, so we don't need you.'*

A fair bit of attention is focused on adolescent suicides because they're a high-risk group, but a similar focus has not been as evident in a similar high-risk group - suicide amongst seniors. People over the age of sixty-five comprise ten percent of the population, but account for fifteen to twenty percent of suicides.

Sometimes seniors can be difficult to deal with especially when many changes are occurring. Quite often they don't hear or see as well, and many suffer serious health problems.

Consider how annoying it is to a sprightly eighty-year-old to have someone talk to them as if they were a young child or mentally disabled. When others talk down to them they get uppity themselves. And even worse, others yell at them and assume they're deaf. They must scramble to turn down their hearing aids (it hurts their ears). Many forget that those who have hearing problems normally wear hearing aids. Don't automatically assume that just because a person has white hair that you must raise the volume of your voice.

Most of us are sensitive to the weather, but with age, the body becomes less able to respond to long exposure to heat or cold. Many feel the cold most during the night when their bodies are in a resting mode; so wear socks to bed at night and require warmer blankets. In cold weather, some older people may develop accidental hypothermia, a drop in internal body temperature (below 35 degrees Celsius) that can be fatal if not detected and treated promptly. In hot, humid weather, a build-up of body heat can cause heat stroke or heat exhaustion (body temperature of 40 degrees Celsius or higher) especially those elderly who have heart and circulatory problems or diabetes.

### I'm so lonely!

*'My sixty-seven-year-old sister is so lonely that she's just pining away and waiting to die. How can I get her kick-started again?'*

Remember that bumper sticker a few years back, *'Have you hugged your kid today?'* Well young adults could be asked, *'Have you phoned your parents today?'* They're wishing you would. A little phone call occasionally to say, *'Mom/Dad, how are you today?'* and having a little chat - is all it would take. Everyone needs to have meaningful, caring relationships with other human beings. If they don't, they may feel tremendous sadness, a sense that nobody cares and feelings of powerlessness. They believe that no one cares for them or understands them, and they express fear and concerns that their families don't love them any more. Even though there doesn't seem to be a lot of hard evidence of that - they still feel that way.

On the other hand, if they're the lonely senior whose kids never call, there's really no need to stay lonely. If they can't get out to meet people, there are people who will come to their home to meet them and sit and chat a while. They're not those kids they miss so much, but they're still wonderful people.

After retirement, one woman felt the need to do something outside the home, so she contacted a senior's outreach group and decided to do something for herself by doing something for others. They put her in touch with two seniors who needed visitors. One couldn't hear very well and was blind and the other was crippled with osteoarthritis. Why did she volunteer? *'There's a lot more to life than playing bingo.'* She said. *'When you give of yourself, you get so much back. All of us have a cross to bear or a mountain to climb and if you have someone to climb it with - it's so much easier. I phone them just about every day and it means so much, because their phone probably wouldn't have rung for days.'*

Encourage your sister to volunteer or join senior's groups so she will have the company she needs to get on with life.

### Grandparenting

Loving grandparents can have a profound impact on their grandchildren. Many grandchildren have gone so far as to say that if it had not been for a loving, understanding grandparent, they don't know how they would have made it this far in life. Some have felt a deeper sense of bonding with a grandparent than with a parent.

Grandparents have three unique resources that can be special gifts to their children's children: time, wisdom and unconditional love. For this to work however, the critical factor is the grandparent's freedom of choice. Unfortunately, some parents take advantage of their own parents in the raising of their young and abuse the privilege of having grandparents nearby. There's a much greater likelihood that grandparents will volunteer their babysitting skills, rather than be expected to baby-sit automatically. Wise children will ask the grandparents when they would like to spend time with their grandchildren - not expect them to fill in whenever they need them.

Some grandparents were not particularly good parents but became remarkably good grandparents. They learned from their mistakes and mellowed through the years. The man who mainly ignored his own children proves to be a doting grandfather, who walks babies by the hour, coos and plays with them to the amazement of everyone.

Some grandparents convince their grandchildren of their genuine love and concern and gently curb them from that which is genuinely harmful and encourage the long-range good. The child knows that their interest is in his or her welfare - not their own - and that their love is deep and genuine.

Some parents, often without realising it, have some unresolved insecurities. Therefore, they may lay expectations and demands on their young offspring that pass on those patterns of insecurity. Grandparents can provide the guidance that can offset these insecurities. Unfortunately, many grandparents live far away from their grandchildren, so might not be able to bond with them as well as they'd like to, but they can still do their bit via mail, e-mail and actual visits.

Grandparents too, have had to adjust to the shift in traditional roles. They now have family units including children, stepchildren, parents and step-parents and all the problems that accompany those relationships. With forty percent of marriages ending in divorce, the role of grandparents is changing. It's unfortunate that some grandparents lose contact with their grandchildren when one parent moves away, or an estranged in-law won't let grandparents have access to the children.

Other grandparents find the opposite and find themselves back in the parenting roll they felt was over when their children grew up. These grandparents find themselves in the middle of the dropping-off-and-picking-up routine when the custodial parent needs economical day care or after-school tending of their children. In many cultures, extended families are the norm and grandparents provide this care, whether the parents divorce or stay together. However, in most modern societies, this just isn't an option because of the distance between grandparents, their children and grandchildren.

Holidays are uniquely difficult for the grandparents of divorced or extended stepfamilies. Grandparents may find themselves in the middle, when the custodial parent re-marries. They may not really like the new parent and find themselves contending with the new spouse's children as well as their own grandchildren. Here are some tips on how to smooth the waters over the holidays when family gatherings bring mixed family groups together:

1. Keep your negative feelings of unease, jealousy (or whatever) in check.

2. Don't go overboard and try too hard. Because it takes some family group five years to click - don't expect miracles. Accept people for what they are, not what you wish they would be.
3. Be willing to compromise; bend with the needs of the entire group.
4. Try to determine the timing of visits long before the holidays.

### Handling a Heart Attack

*'My husband's brother, aged 67, suffered a heart attack last month. He is recovering nicely, but his heart attack has put a serious damper on my own sex life. You see, his brother had been making love to his wife when he had his heart attack. My husband is just a couple of years younger than his brother and has high blood pressure, so is very reluctant to have sex with me.'*

A recent medical study confirms that it's highly unlikely that sexual activity would bring on a heart attack. Sex is about as risky as getting angry or waking up in the morning. Heavy exertion can be three times riskier than any of those activities. And sex did not increase the heart attack risk at all among patients who exercised regularly. Another study said that those men who died of heart attacks during sex were more likely to be with someone other than their wives. The element of danger apparently was more than the heart could handle.

*'Last month my wife had a heart attack. She's home from the hospital now, but I find I don't sleep well at night. I haven't talked to her about it, but I'm afraid that I'll wake up some morning and find her dead in the bed beside me.'*

This is understandable in the circumstances. Speak to her doctor to see how she's really doing and whether your fears are warranted. Take a CPR (coronary pulmonary resuscitation) course so you can act if she has another heart attack. Then if necessary, you can do your best to revive her while waiting for ambulance attendants.

If you must leave your wife alone even for short periods of time, you might get her an alert system that she wears around her neck that can summon help in seconds. This will not only make you feel better but will make her feel as if she has more control if there is another emergency.

### Elderly Non-verbal Messages

If you were to visit the average nursing home, you'd probably find:

- Those who are bedridden often stroke their covers or,

- The more mobile seniors stroke a velvet chair or some other soft fabric.

Many seniors miss out on the luxury of having others touch them. In nursing homes, patients receive attention from the staff, but how often does anyone touch them in a loving way. There's a tremendous difference between *being looked after and being cared for*. When relatives and friends come to visit, many don't realise how important it is for them to hold the person's hand, touch their arm or give them a hug to show they care.

We all have a life-long need for affectionate touching and caring from others. If an older person becomes cranky or miserable, one of the reasons could be that this necessity of life is missing from their lives.

*'I often visit my mother at the seniors' home. For some reason, I feel very edgy when I'm around one of the male residents, but don't understand why. He seems all right – but something in me tells me to be cautious around him. What's happening to cause this reaction?'*

Occasionally, when we read another person's body language, another non-verbal communication skill kicks in. Women call this skill intuition. Most men call it their *"gut reaction"* or they have a *"hunch"*. Suddenly, they have the feeling that they really should – or should not – do something, although they can't identify why they feel that way. They try to find facts to explain their feeling, but they often can't.

Many of us scoff at this flash of information and discount our intuitive feelings because we can't find any facts to back up our reactions. For instance, you find yourself suddenly feeling uncomfortable around another person. You may even feel threatened and yet when you consciously examine the person, you can't determine why you feel your unease.

I had this phenomenon explained this way. Our conscious brain (which I call my brain's computer software) keeps up-to-date data available for easy reference. Our subconscious brain (our hard drive) is far superior to the conscious brain because it holds all our memories - those we consciously remember and those buried in the back recesses of our minds.

Should you be listening to your intuitive feelings? Of course, you should! When intuition tells you something - listen - because it's seldom wrong. You can probably recall when something about a person upset you and your instincts said to watch out. You may or may not have listened to these instincts and probably suffered the consequences.

The only time I haven't listened to my intuitive feelings was when I took an instant dislike to a person. After standing back and analysing why I felt this way, I realised that this person physically resembled another person I disliked and distrusted. By turning off my intuitive feelings, I learned that the person was all right.

I remember an incident when my intuition kicked in. While driving, I was passing some parked cars and thought I saw some movement in front of one of them, but as I came closer did not see anything. However, I felt the need to stop and check it out. What I found has haunted me for years – what I saw crawling out from behind the parked car (and would have been right in front of my wheels as I passed) was a baby crawling on the road. I put my emergency flashers on my car and tried to determine where the baby had come from I followed the direction it had come from and saw a sidewalk leading to stairs and an open front door to a home. I picked up the baby and went to the door, rang the bell and was greeted by a young woman who stared at me holding her baby and asked, *'What are you doing with my baby?'*

I pointed to my car and told her the story. She thanked me profusely and promised that she would put a lock on the door, so the baby could not sneak out again.

You might talk to the nursing staff at the home to explain your feelings and get their response as to whether there is some reason for your cautious approach to this person.

### *Learning a New Skill*

Seniors may have problems learning how to perform new tasks. When teaching someone a new skill (such as how to run a wheelchair lift for a disabled mate) you might run into serious objections. Being able to teach others takes talent and perseverance. Using paraphrasing will help you implant information. Knowing that people pass through four definite stages when learning something new might help.

These four stages are:

a) This is where the person isn't even aware that they lack the skill. (They may not have been aware that such an item as a wheelchair lift exists).

b) The person is aware that they lack the skill. (They know they haven't learned how to manage a wheelchair lift).

c) The person now knows the techniques of the skill but must stop and think before s/he before s/he reacts. *('Let me think, do have to make sure the ramp is down before I push this button?')*

d) The skill is now well established and automatic. The person probably doesn't even think about what s/he's doing – s/he's on *"automatic pilot"*.

It's good to remember that it takes a younger person, six weeks to *'lock in'* how to do something a new way and up to three months to *'lock-in'* doing something a different way. In the elderly, this can take possibly twice as long. Be patient.

People of all ages resist change, but the most resistant are the elderly. It's comfortable doing things the old way and many fear they might not succeed at doing things a new way. For instance, as their children grow and move away, elderly couples find their home is too large, but balk at moving. One or both may retire, and this involves more changes. Others become disabled and still others need to adjust to living without their mate. These situations can be frightening - because they involve change. These changes range from finding a smaller home to finding a closer supermarket to do their shopping.

People go through four basic stages when they're forced to change anything they do. There's a considerable amount of temptation to slip back to doing things the old way. Knowing these stages can help you keep them on track.

These four stages are:

1. **Unfreezing:** This happens when you *"unfreeze"* a regular way of doing things, which allows the person to accept new ideas. This involves breaking down of old ways of doing things and can involve customs and traditions.

2. **Changing:** This provides a new pattern of behaviour and identifies a new way of doing something. For instance, a man would like to do his neighbour's shopping for him, rather than having his neighbour walk several blocks carrying groceries. He may run into resistance. To overcome the neighbour's resistance to his offer, he would have to identify the driving and restraining forces for the change. He should be ready for any objections he expects his neighbour will make about his attempts to help him.

3.  **Refreezing:** The new idea replaces the old one and the new way is *"frozen"* so the person isn't tempted to revert to the old way. A die-hard will try to go back to doing it the old way, so you must be wary of him slipping back to his old routines.
4.  **Commitment:** People are ready to make plans that utilise the new way.

### *Not Important any more!*

Just getting up in the morning is a chore for many seniors. The main causes are that they feel there's no meaning to their lives, they have nothing to get up for and have nothing to stimulate them into action. Depression is often the result.

When depression sets in - it triggers other responses. Suddenly people feel every ache and pain that can escalate into serious disabilities. Life takes on special meaning when seniors like what they're doing and have a good relationship with their friends and family. They seldom complain about their aches and pains.

Happy seniors are busy seniors. This mental and physical activity results in better mental and physical health that inevitably eliminates most of the daily aches and pains that plague the elderly. Society is giving considerable effort to keep seniors active, happy and productive. Those employed in the recreational and travel areas will find their occupations becoming more and more valuable. This is due to the rising percentage of seniors who are truly living and enjoying their retirement.

### *Lives in the Past*

Many seniors live in the past. They'll talk for hours about their childhood - but may not give the attention required to living in the present. Some believe that their past will always influence what happens in their future. They may use this as an excuse to avoid changing their behaviour.

Many people in this group state, *'I'm too old... Not smart enough... Not good at that.'* These people are stating, *'I'm a finished product in this area and I'm never going to be different.'*

Talk with them and identify what you see them doing to themselves. Ask their permission to bring it to their attention when you hear them running themselves down or living in the past.

If life doesn't come up to their expectations because of lack of insight on their part, they should console themselves that it's never too late for conditions to change. Although they may have missed some opportunities during their youth, each phase of life brings its own compensations for those who seek them. They simply need faith that everything will go right. Instead of dwelling in the past, encourage them to concentrate their energy on building a better, happier life for themselves and make the most of their present good moments.

If they persist, suggest that they put a loose elastic band around their wrist and snap it (ouch) every time they catch themselves using this type of destructive thinking. This negative reinforcement will keep them from dwelling on the past. We are and become what we think - so encourage them to think positively!

### *Osteoporosis*

*'My wife has just been diagnosed as having osteoporosis. How dangerous is this and is there anything she can do to treat it?'*

Osteoporosis literally means *"porous bones"*. Through gradual thinning and weakening, bones that were once strong become lighter and more fragile. In advanced ages, bones resemble a laced honeycomb.

Osteoporosis can affect any adult, but it is most common and much more severe in women. For this reason, all women should pay special attention to the changes their bodies undergo as they age. One in every four women over sixty is affected by this disorder. Because it develops silently and generally painlessly over several years, it may go unnoticed until some bones break. Women who are fair skinned, are thin and have a small frame are more susceptible than larger, heavier people or if they have a family history of osteoporosis. Loss of height or broken bones are usually the first real signs of this disorder. The *"dowager's hump"* or hunchback often accompanies osteoporosis.

Those who lament the fact that their hair has gone grey too soon may have more than aesthetics to worry about. Premature greying could be a sign of osteoporosis. A study of men and women conducted by U.S. researchers found that those with premature greying (their hair had turned more than fifty per cent grey by age forty) who had no other identifiable risk factors - were 4.4 times more likely to have osteoporosis than those who were not pre-maturely grey. The researchers suggest it's possible that a gene for premature greying may be adjacent to or linked with the gene that determines peak bone mass.

It's an interesting observation - an additional risk factor to look for when determining the risk of osteoporosis.

No treatment except preventative can alleviate the onset of osteoporosis. However, your wife should be encouraged to increase her calcium intake by eating dairy products, dark green, leafy vegetables and salmon, sardines and oysters. To slow the rate of bone loss her doctor may recommend an estrogen supplement and regular exercise such as walking, jogging and bicycle riding. Fluoride may increase bone density. A combination of calcium, vitamin D, estrogen and fluoride are being tested in hopes of finding a way to stop bone loss.

### Sticky-iffies (Backhanded Compliments)

Sometimes people in authority or elderly can be very hurtful with their comments. They do this by giving the recipient a sticky-iffy. Sticky-iffies occur when they start their comments by giving a compliment. Then, they immediately discount their positive statement, by adding something negative. This completely nullifies the compliment and leaves the person feeling wounded.

Others use disguised or obvious put-downs that are meant to hurt. For example:

* *'You're pretty young to be a supervisor, aren't you?'*
* *'Every time I take a taxi, it's always people from Asia who are driving. Can't you people find anything else to do except drive taxis?'*
* *'You're earning a good salary for a woman.'*

When dealing with these people use the following formula:

1.  After receiving the sticky-iffy or put-down, reflect your understanding of the situation. Say, *'You feel/think/believe...'* which confirms that you heard what they said to you (a form of paraphrasing).
2.  Then state, *'I understand / perceive / appreciate / empathise with / realise...'* then express their point of view, as you perceive it.
3.  State, *'I think/feel/believe/have...'* and state your beliefs about the topic. Don't start your statement with such words as *'but, however, although or nevertheless.'*
4.  Ask an open question (one that can't be answered by, *'yes'* or *'no.'*) An example relating to discriminatory statements regarding age:

They say, *'You're very young to be a supervisor, aren't you?'*
You say, *'You feel that I'm too young to be a supervisor?'*
They say, *'Well you are young!'*
You say, *'I think I understand what you're saying. I feel I fill the requirements for the position I'm holding. I have six years' experience in this department, have a B.A. degree and have completed all the supervisory training provided by our company. What other prerequisites do you feel I need to handle my position?'*

Tone of voice is very important in these exchanges. Your voice should not show defensiveness but show that you're stating facts. This starts a dialogue where you can discuss the facts rather than display emotions.

An example relating to racial slurs: They say, *'Every time I take a taxi, it's always people from Asia who are driving. Can't you people find anything else to do except drive taxis?'*

You say, *'You feel that people from Asia should have jobs other than driving a taxi. I realise why you must believe that. Many people from my country need to get extra education to work at their usual occupations in your country. I'm taking university courses and will soon be working in my normal type of job. What kind of special courses did you take to work in your type of job?'*

A gender-related example: They say, *'You're earning a good salary for a woman.'*

You say, *'You believe that women should earn less than men?'*
They say, *'Yes, I do.'*
You say, *'I appreciate what you're saying. I believe women deserve an equal chance to earn the same kind of salary as men. Women pay rent like men, pay the same for food as men and pay taxes like men. What are the reasons for your belief that women should earn less than men?'*

Use this technique for any sticky-iffy comments and disguised or obvious put-downs.

### Condescending Attitude

*'How do I deal with seniors who are condescending to me - treat me like dirt? My next-door neighbour is very rude to me. When my husband and I are out in our back yard, he acts as if I'm not there and directs all*

*his comments to my husband. When he does speak to me, he gives me the impression that because I'm a housewife, I know nothing.'*

This kind of person is not very self-assured him/herself. They try to put you down, to make themselves feel more important. They may or may not use sarcasm to do this. Turn off your defence mechanism and try to learn *"inside"* information about what he likes to talk about. Then, surprise him with your knowledge of the subject.

If all else fails, confront him by saying, *'When you and Jim were discussing the middle-east crisis and I mentioned that I had just heard an announcement on the radio about the latest developments, you immediately changed the topic. You've done this in several of our past conversations. This made me feel that you thought what I had to say was not important. Can you tell me why you did that?'*

This is rather confrontational, but this kind of person sometimes needs a show of power to make them pay attention. If he retaliates with, *'Pretty touchy, aren't you?'*

Reply, *'How would you react if someone did that to you?'*

Whatever he replies, say, *'I'll have to remember that the next time you're rude to me.'* and end the conversation. Realise that **you** are in control of the situation (no matter what their attitude shows). Don't allow them to get beneath your veneer and make you *"lose your cool"*. Ask yourself whether this person is worth the aggravation of continued exposure.

### *Grieving*

*'My neighbour's wife passed away recently, and her husband is having a terrible time adjusting to her death. Although he's in good physical shape, he's suffering emotionally. How can our family help him through this?'*

Death is often the worst psychological trauma people will ever face. Those who must deal with a death may feel both grief and depression. The difference between grief and depression is; depression is a medical diagnosis and grief is a natural growth process. And if he tries to avoid grieving, he will get depressed. Grief is not a point event. A funeral is a point event – something that happens on a specific day at a specific time with a beginning and an end. Some people have grief that lasts for weeks. Some have grief that is never resolved. Some people have a deep grief, while others appear to not have grief by comparison. There's quite a difference from a point event and the long process of grief that is very much an individual reaction.

Most of us don't know how to comfort a grieving friend. First pay attention to what your instincts say. If your first impulse is to phone or visit him, don't put it off by the fear that you might be intruding on his privacy. He'll probably appreciate your concern. Let him know how very sorry you are, but don't use phrases like, *'I know just how you feel,'* unless you've very recently lost a close loved one yourself.

Listen carefully to what he says. If he reveals that he doesn't know how he'll get through the days without his loved one - resist the desire to cheer him up or offer advice. What he requires right now is the opportunity of talking about his concerns - not on you providing answers.

Resist statement such as *'Don't feel that way.'* Or, *'This feeling is only temporary; the situation will improve with time.'* Many grieving people feel they should have done something to prevent the loved one's death, so there's an element of guilt. Telling him that his feelings are wrong may only cause him to bury his feelings instead of resolving them.

People grieve, not only because a close friend or relative has died, but because of any serious loss. They grieve because a good friend moves away, they're laid off or fired from a job they love, they lose a limb, their eyesight or hearing, they have a financial disaster, a romantic relationship breaks up, they divorce or lose custody of their children.

The pain can be intense, but no matter what the loss, the grieving process remains the same. The only part that changes is the degree of grief the person suffers. The six stages of the grieving process can last varying lengths of time.

These stages are:

- An overwhelming feeling of loss;
- Shock and denial; (*'This couldn't be happening to me!'*) Even if the death has been expected - they cannot believe it.
- Emotional upheaval; (mood-swings and depression) *'There are all kinds of things I wanted to say to her, that I never said to her.'*
- Withdrawal; (lick their wounds in solitude).
- Understanding of loss; (acceptance).
- Hope (things will get better).

146

Death is always sudden. It happens in a heartbeat. It doesn't matter how much warning you may have. It doesn't matter how much you know or how relieved you are that the illness is over. When death finally happens, it always happens in a heartbeat. It's always sudden - always a shock. The first cycle of grief is an annual cycle. It's not anything biological. It may only have to do with things social - the various things that mark the progress of time through a year. We have Christmas and Easter, anniversaries: we have all those events. And whatever we did, we must adjust to it.

One of the hardest things people have with grief is expressing their anger. They don't want to speak ill of the dead. Some are very angry that the person died before they were ready for it to happen. However, if they don't acknowledge their anger, it's just going to eat holes in their gut and it's going to take longer for them to get over the grieving cycle.

Those suffering from grief may put up barricades to hide their feelings from others and may need reassuring words before they'll let others comfort them physically. For example: At a funeral, a close family friend tries to comfort the grieving person. They try to give the person a hug but find the person rigid and unresponsive and appears to push them away. What's happening here? If you were offering condolences, you might feel hurt by this perceived sign of rejection. You wonder if you should pursue and keep offering your support or should you back off and let the person grieve in private.

What's likely happening is the grieving person may feel too vulnerable to trust others with their feelings. They're afraid they'll *"fall apart"* if they feel one *more* strong emotion. Therefore, they seem to repel others and physically push others away or remain rigid when others try to comfort them. If you're a close friend or relative, please don't give up - watch for non-verbal signs that they're ready for and need comforting.

At later visits with the person, try again to see if they're past their emotional upheaval. Watch their body language and reactions. If you perceive that they're still hurting and appear to need comforting, put your hand on their arm. If they don't pull away, put your hand on their shoulder. Again, if they don't pull away, attempt again to give them a hug expressing your wish to comfort them. When the person is ready for comforting, they'll show you by their reaction. Many may finally allow themselves to sob and cry, knowing that there's someone else available to help them through their sorrow.

Some may never allow others to comfort them physically - they're not comfortable with hugs and physical signs of affection. Keep voicing your support and do all those little things that show how much you care about them. Just having your strength nearby might be what they need to progress through the grieving process. Nobody should have to handle this transition alone. Be there when they need you.

Unfortunately, forty percent of elderly male widowers are likely to die within one year of their spouse's deaths. One research study found that if a man doesn't marry within the first two years of losing his wife - death is often inevitable. This can be attributed to the fact that a lot of them were workaholics and the woman was his anchor to the outside world.

Younger men suffering from the early demise of their partners often jump quickly into another relationship or marriage that often results in disaster. Men suffer inwardly and silently. Elderly men who've lost a spouse have usually lost the most significant person in their lives. They traditionally don't talk to anybody about their emotional issues other than their wife - if that. If they lose their wife - they've lost everything.

Many have never looked after a home before and their wives usually looked after the social side of things, cultivating the family and friend relationships. The widower is left not knowing what to do. Some men find there's no meaning left in their life – so they give up and literally die of a broken heart.

Most women take up to four years to mourn a spouse and readjust to their new life. Men turn around faster, usually because they've pushed their grief aside and haven't dealt with their loss. They immerse themselves in their work and keep their emotions to themselves. They're in a highly emotional state. Many people have affairs or take new partners that are totally different than the one they've lost. They should never do anything like move to a new home, take on a new partner or find a new job for at least a year after the death of a spouse.

Here are some steps people can take to deal with life after the death of a spouse. Encourage your neighbour to do the following:

- Seek bereavement support either through a counsellor or a self-help group.

- Get financial counselling and advice from a variety of sources.
- Seek out groups and activities that interest him.
- Develop household management skills - some men take cooking classes that can have added social benefits.
- Contact his nearest community centre or local health unit and ask about becoming involved in their wellness programs.
- Allow himself to *"waste time"* - to savour the pleasure of the present and to live for the moment.
- Be good to himself and indulge in a day of golf, a night at a play or dinner with a friend.

### Alzheimer's Disease

*'I'm sure my neighbour (who lives alone) has Alzheimer's disease. She's displaying unusual behaviour and I'm concerned about her welfare. She seems to have a "blank" look about her and has started to shuffle when she walks. Just last year, she participated in acquasise classes, baked for the neighbourhood kids and was very active in the community. But lately, I've noticed that she mainly stays at home.*

*'The last time I visited her, I noticed how dishevelled she looked and how untidy her home now appears. She has a dog and I heard him howling with the cold when we had our last storm. I had to go over and ring her doorbell to ask her to take him in. I'm concerned about her welfare. Could she possibly have Alzheimer's disease or is she just getting old? How do I know whether she has Alzheimer's or not and how can I help her if she does have the disease?'*

Doctors still can't determine completely whether a person has Alzheimer's disease until the person dies. They can guess - but they don't know for sure until an autopsy is completed. But there are many signs they watch for that point in that direction.

For instance, people suffering from Alzheimer's disease have difficulty communicating with others. They may not be able to make themselves understood or they don't understand what others are saying. They may become angry or defensive if they can't find the words to respond to others' questions. They forget within seconds even information they might have understood at the time it was said. Others can read words but fail to understand the meaning of the words. They might understand what you say if you're right in front of them but fail to understand you when speaking to you on the telephone. Those who were very articulate or had the ability to put words to paper suddenly don't know how to

149

find the words and even if they find the words, they forget how to write them down.

Unfortunately, many forget that those who have the disease may understand more than they can state. Please don't talk about them as if they aren't there.

Another serious problem surfaces when they lose their sense of direction. Many become lost even in their own neighbourhoods or homes. The route they took to the corner store is suddenly unfamiliar to them. They forget where their bedroom fits into the layout of their homes. They try to put cakes into the dishwasher to bake, milk into the cupboard and sugar into the fridge. (We've all done the last two, but with Alzheimer's patients, this can be part of the overall pattern - not just an isolated incident).

Alzheimer's patients often live in the past and think their sons (who may resemble their fathers) *are* their long-departed husbands and talk to them as if they are. Others lose things and can become very agitated because they believe someone has stolen the articles from them. After one woman was diagnosed, her family packed up her belongings and found money hidden all over the apartment. Their mother had insisted that others had been stealing from her. In this woman's cupboard were fifteen boxes of tea. The local grocer stated that every time she came into the store, she purchased tea (because she forgot that she had already bought some the day before).

Often family members miss identifying the early signs of this chronic and destructive condition. Some signs can be the person's difficulty remembering recent information, losing track of time, frequent forgetfulness and disorientation. While everyone forgets things now and then, the person with Alzheimer's disease begins to lose the ability to retain new information. Memories of high school may be very clear, but present events are forgotten.

Some become dangerous to themselves and others. One woman who lived in an apartment was forced to obtain her neighbour's help because she had become lost in her apartment when she got up at night to use the bathroom. Somehow, she had gone through the main door to her apartment and it had locked behind her. Twice, another senior almost set his apartment on fire, first by leaving something on the stove, then when he dropped a lighted cigarette on the couch. Thankfully, someone had been visiting him at the time.

Alzheimer's is a degenerative disease of the brain's nerve cells that results in a progressive loss of memory and thinking abilities. Its onset is usually seen in those sixty and older, but there are also cases of it beginning as young as forty.

Family members should begin considering Alzheimer's if they notice the affected person has difficulty keeping on schedule, taking their medication, eating regularly or knowing the time or day of the week. If these indicators happen - a medical evaluation becomes crucial. This can include such things as a complete medical history including all conditions and medications and a complete neurological examination to assess thinking ability.

If the above symptoms describe your neighbour, try to contact her family, her doctor or any other person who may have a vested interest in her welfare. She may be in deep trouble and not be able to help herself. See that she gets the help she needs. If there isn't anyone close to her, contact your local Alzheimer's Society or Mental Health Clinic so they can do an assessment of her needs.

There is some hope on the horizon for women relating to Alzheimer's disease. Women who take estrogen supplements after age 70 are less likely to suffer from dementia caused by the non-familial form of Alzheimer's disease. In females, estrogen facilitates the formation of synapses – biochemical connections between nerve cells in the brain. In males, testosterone is the facilitator. Women's estrogen levels drop after menopause, but men's testosterone levels remain about the same until their 70s or 80s, which explains why women over 70 are three times more likely to suffer from dementia than men of the same age.

### Dangerous Inaccessibility

*'A couple I know live in a high-rise condominium building and they find that when they enter the building, others try to "piggy-back" and get in without a key. This violates the security practices of their building. As the wife is small and elderly, she doesn't know whether she should take the chance of endangering herself by confronting them or whether she should just say nothing.'*

If the person looks like the sort she could deal with, she should explain to them that she couldn't let others into the building - that it's a breach of the security rules of the building. Ask them to buzz their party on the intercom if they want to visit someone in the building.

If the person or persons appear menacing, she should go immediately to her resident manager. If these people take an elevator, she should watch to see which floor they go to, so she has an idea where they've gone in the building. If the resident manager isn't there and she feels the people might be in the building for criminal reasons, she should call the police immediately.

One senior related, *'I had a frightening situation happen to me last month. I live in an apartment complex that has an intercom for entry into the building. Because youngsters played with the intercom during the night and bothered us so often, the management decided to have the main door to the building locked at 11:00 pm. This meant that if anyone wanted to visit someone in the building after that time, they couldn't contact him or her through the intercom. Instead, they'd have to phone their friends and their friends would have to come down and physically let them into the building.*

*'This appeared to work well, until I became ill after midnight one night, when the rest of my family were away on holidays. I called and asked for an ambulance. They kept me on the line and became concerned when they found the ambulance drivers could not get into the building. It took over half an hour for them to gain entry to the building and this was only because a tenant came home and opened the door.*

*'The day after, our building managers installed a lock box with a key to the building, just outside the main doors. Police and fire officials were the only ones with keys to this lock box. This would allow emergency services personnel to gain entry to our building after hours.'*

For those of you who live in facilities that lock the main doors at night, you should consider this alternative in case of an emergency.

### Handicapped Parking

*'I really get upset when I see an able-bodied person parking in spots identified as handicapped parking. My friend is handicapped, and he often finds that able-bodied people park in the handicapped spots. I've resorted to printing up cards that I place on their windshield telling them in no uncertain terms what I think about their parking in those spots. What else could I do about this?'*

It's possible that the person *is* handicapped. Hearing impaired people can also park in handicapped spots. Most municipalities insist that handicapped people display either a license plate or sticker proving they <u>are</u> handicapped.

If they're not handicapped, call your local police and they'll tow the car away. The person will likely be given a warning or a traffic ticket.

Another complaint handicapped people have against others, is that they're treated as a non-entity. Others talk to the companion of the person in the wheelchair, instead of the person in the chair. Many people in wheelchairs don't receive eye contact from others - in fact most people do anything but give them eye contact. This put-down makes them feel as if they're invisible. Even the most severely disabled or handicapped person should be given eye contact.

### *Hidden Drug Abuser?*

Could the seniors in your life be hidden drug abusers? Here's an example of how one senior ended up abusing antibiotics.

He realised that he had a vicious case of strep throat, so finally went to see his doctor who prescribed ampicillin, to be taken three times a day for ten days. However, after only four days, he felt much better - so stopped taking it. A week later when his sore throat recurred, he took the rest of the ampicillin and his symptoms again ceased. Ten days later, he became sick again and got a new prescription for ampicillin.

This is a classic antibiotics abuse. By cutting his treatment short and then self-prescribing a second, inadequate dose of the drug, he may have reduced the drug's effectiveness. If only enough medicine is taken to kill the most susceptible germs, the hardy handful can survive to grow new colonies. This new batch of bacteria will be more resistant to the medication and an additional exposure to too short a dosage of antibiotic could again kill all but the hardiest of this hardier bunch - producing an even more resistant strain.

People still believe that antibiotics are harmless miracle drugs. It's estimated that up to half of all antibiotic use is either unnecessary or inappropriate. When faced with penicillin-resistant infections, doctors often opt to prescribe a more powerful broad-spectrum antibiotic that mows down both good and bad bacteria. So, it's critical that prescriptions be used at the correct dosage for the entire period prescribed and not be stockpiled for future use.

### English as a second language

*'My elderly neighbour is Chinese and comes from a decidedly different cultural background than me. I try hard to understand what he's saying, but I often can't understand him. He has the same problem understanding me. What can I do about this problem?'*

If there are younger people in his home, ask them to interpret for him. If he lives alone, check your city/town to see if there is a translation service available that can provide a three-way conversation where they can provide translation for you both.

People, whose second language is English, normally go through a complicated process until they become completely fluent in English:

**Stage 1:** They hear what you say in English.
**Stage 2:** They mentally translate what you've said into their mother tongue.
**Stage 3:** They mentally construct their answer in their own language.
**Stage 4:** They mentally translate it into English.
**Stage 5:** They give you a verbal reply in English.

You can see that this process takes time, so if you're conversing with someone whose second language is English, try to:

1. Use common language. You can't expect them to learn jargon or technical language right away.
2. Allow them time to go through the stages of interpretation to determine what you've said. The "pregnant pause" between the end of your talking and the beginning of their answering, may be necessary for complete understanding on their part.
3. Watch their body language. If they give a helpless look or shrug their shoulders, you've lost them. Repeat what you've said, trying different and more simplistic words.

Your neighbour too has a responsibility to try to lessen the problem. He can do his part by attending *"English as a Second Language"* classes.

### Emotional Problems

*'My neighbour lives alone and I don't see her very often, so was surprised to see how much weight she had lost, and she snapped at me*

*when I spoke to her. She looks very depressed and I don't know how I can help her.'*

Now and again we all fly off the handle, feel inferior, suffer from guilt and normally these feelings don't cause problems, however there are signs that show us that seniors are in trouble when they show:

- Helplessness and dependency: Letting others make all the decisions, feel they're unable to do things on their own or letting others do too many things for them.
- Hypochondria: They worry terribly and imagine they're sick, suffering from fatal illnesses or worry about even minor physical ailments, which are clearly non-existent.
- Excessive sullenness: Feeling depressed nearly all the time; that nothing in life is worth doing and has even considered suicide.
- Poor emotional control: frequently becomes excitable or emotional over unimportant matters, angry outbursts or temper tantrums. Are quarrelsome for no reason at all.
- Live in a fantasy world: Spending a lot of time daydreaming, blocking out any real problems.
- Are self-centred: Are unable to share their belongings, are selfish, putting themselves first and believe the world revolves around them.
- Suspicious and mistrusting: Thinks that others are dishonest, will take advantage of them and that life is only full of disappointments, obstacles and frustrations.
- Repeatedly can't sleep, are constantly tired and feel run down or find it hard to get up in the morning.
- Anxious: Worry excessively about little things, are very apprehensive about their future and are afraid to make decisions.

For most of the milder symptoms, having a sympathetic person to listen: a doctor, relative, neighbour, friend or social worker helps. For others that are more serious - having them speak to their family doctor or nearest mental health clinic is the answer.

### Getting medical help

*'I've been helping an elderly neighbour by taking him shopping and to his medical appointments. Several times after he's seen his doctor, he's*

155

*been very agitated. He explained that he didn't think his doctor listens to him and seems to brush him off when he asks questions. Do you think I should go in with him when he sees the doctor?'*

Ask him if this is what he wants you to do or if he wants your help in dealing with his problems. If he agrees, have him write a list of the questions he wants to ask his doctor. Rehearse with him what he should say if the doctor doesn't answer his questions or tries to rush him out the door. If he tries to brush off his questions or seems to be rushing your neighbour out the door, encourage him to stay seated and say, *'You're rushing me. This makes me feel very frustrated because it seems like you're giving me the brush-off by not giving me time to ask my questions. I'd like you to give me time to get the answers I need before I go.'*

In this exchange, he's using feedback:

a) **The problem** – *'He gives your neighbour the brush-off and doesn't give him the information he needs.'*

b) Your neighbour's **feelings or reactions** – *'The doctor's actions frustrate him.'*

c) **Solution** – *'He asks his doctor to give him time to have all his questions answered.'*

Most people will change undesired behaviour if it's brought to their attention in a kind, non-threatening way. But there are exceptions to the rule. Some just don't care what you think, so if the doctor doesn't answer his questions, you would step in on his behalf. As a last resort, you may need to find him a doctor who will listen to him.

### Friend diagnosed with cancer

*'My best friend is 56 and has just been diagnosed with cancer of the pancreas. I want to be there for him while he goes through his ordeal. How can I best help him?'*

Often people withdraw - not because they can't cope or don't care - but because they don't know what to do and are afraid of doing the wrong thing. Here are some things you can do to help your friend through his crisis:

• Don't treat him differently - he's the same person. Some cancer cells may be running wild in his body, but he still likes to live life to the fullest - to laugh, go to football games and talk to friends.

156

- Ask how he is - He may not always want to talk about his illness or the treatment he's receiving, so keep asking him, *'How are you and how are things going?'*

- Be there when he needs you - A phone call, a visit or even a short letter or e-mail is all it takes. He needs your friendship and the support of all his family and friends. He gets tired of being strong all the time especially when he's having a day where things aren't going well.

- Don't just offer help - be there. It's not good enough to offer help – be there without being asked. If you see something you might be able to do for him - suggest it. His life has been turned upside down and he often doesn't have the time to handle daily life. Offer to drive him to his chemotherapy or radiation sessions and hold his head when he's ill after his treatments. Nothing's worse than going through such trauma alone.

- Support his family - not just him. They're going through this as well and need as much (if not more) tender loving care. Ask them what you can do and be a confidant when they need to talk to someone about what they're going through. Drive his children to their basketball practices - take over where he can't be there for his children. Bring food - often his wife is too rushed to prepare all the meals.

It all boils down to - what would you want your friends to do, if you were the one diagnosed with cancer. Use that as your guideline to your actions.

### *I want to stay in my home!*

*'I live alone in the home my husband and I shared for more than thirty years. Lately, I've needed more help with daily chores. What worries me, is that several of my friends have fallen and I'm deathly afraid that I'll fall too. I dread losing my independence but fear it's inevitable that I move into a nursing home.'*

That's not necessarily true. Although many seniors require some help with bathing, dressing, walking, eating and using the toilet, this doesn't appear to be the case with you. Major studies have repeatedly shown that exercise programs can significantly make elderly people of all ages more fit and improve their balance. At age sixty, muscle strength begins to decrease. Exercise that involves weights can reduce this loss. It can increase muscle size and helps with balance, climbing stairs, getting out of bed and raising from a chair.

Usually home is where the heart is, so if you can manage by staying in your own home, do so. If you require more help and don't want to involve your family, consider hiring a part-time aide who can do your heavier chores and shopping. You might consider purchasing a special alert system that's available (worn around your neck or wrist) that you can push if you get into serious difficulty. These are often supplied by emergency services personnel who would come if you needed them. Another solution is to share your home with another senior. This way you'll have someone available if you fall or become ill. This will lessen the need for your family to become involved on a day-to-day basis.

Always keep in mind, that the more you can do for yourself, the more independence you'll keep. A good exercise program should be first on your *"to do"* list to make sure you keep active enough to keep your independence. Another key to proper health and independence is maintaining an active lifestyle. Get out socially and live it up!

### My wife is smothering me!

*'My wife is smothering me! This is the second marriage for both of us (we're both in our 60s). She has not worked away from the home since we married five years ago. She's so dependent on me that it's making me want to stay away from our home. She waits all day for me to come home from work and monopolises my time so much that I have no privacy whatsoever. I've told her repeatedly that she's smothering me, and I've asked her for some `space' - but she won't listen to me. What do I have to do - threaten to leave her before she hears me?'*

This is a form of passive behaviour. Dependent people believe that they should be dependent on others and must have someone stronger on whom to rely. Dependency causes greater dependency, failure to learn and insecurity, since one is at the mercy of those on whom one depends.

Most dependent adults grew up in homes where the parents taught their children to be dependent and to lean on them. Women from these homes usually switch their dependency to their husbands when they marry. This is an almost automatic response. If she had lived on her own before her marriage, she'd likely have lost her dependent nature.

Encourage her to refuse help unless it's necessary. Help her know that risks - while possibly resulting in failures - are worth taking and failing is not a catastrophe. When she asks you for help in making a decision - stop yourself from doing so. Instead ask her, *'What do you think you should do?'* Nine times out of ten, she'll know what she should do – she just wants confirmation. When she realises that she knew what to do all along, she'll see that she can make more decisions by herself.

Your wife needs encouragement from you to see that she has an independent life of her own. Unfortunately, she went right from her parents' home into her first marriage. Her passive behaviour keeps her from attempting independent action. Try sending her to assertiveness training or buy her some books on the topic. You might suggest that she get a job outside the home or become a volunteer to help her make independent decisions.

# CHAPTER 7

## DEALING WITH DIFFICULT PARENTS

### *What is a Father?*

*A father is forced to endure childbirth without the benefit of an anaesthetic.*

*A father growls when he feels good and laughs aloud when he's scared half to death.*

*A father never feels worthy of the worship in a child's eyes. He's never quite the hero his daughter thinks; never quite the man his son believed him to be and this worries him.*

*So, he works too hard to try and smooth the rough places in the road for those of his own who will follow him.*

*Fathers are what give daughters away to other men who are not nearly good enough, so they can have grandchildren who are smarter than anybody's.*

*Fathers make bets with insurance companies about who'll live the longest. One day they lose, and the bets are paid off to the part of them they leave behind.*

*I don't know where fathers go when they die. But I have an idea that after a good rest wherever they are, they just won't sit on a cloud and wait for the women they loved and the children they bore. They'll be busy there too, repairing the stairs, oiling the gate, improving the streets and smoothing the way.*

### *What is a Mother?*

*A mother is forced to go through nine months while incubating an infant.*

*A mother goes through the agonies of childbirth often without anaesthetic.*

*A mother winces when her child first crawls, and walks knowing the injuries these skills can bring.*

*A mother feeds her toddler several times a day knowing that both she and the toddler will likely need a bath or thorough wash after each episode.*

*A mother allows her children to leave the safety of her nest to go to school - knowing that there are possible predators out there.*

*A mother sighs and sheds many tears, when her children go off to college, get married or move away from home.*

*Mothers always remain mothers and even when we are middle-aged ourselves, we still lean on her for advice and sympathy.*

*When mothers greet their female friends in heaven, their conversation
normally begins with 'And how are the kids?'*

### Parents are for life

Sharing and caring for each other takes a nosedive when families stop
using common courtesy and everyday manners with each other. Why
don't they treat family members with the same courtesy they give to
their friends and even strangers? They drift into it - because of bad
habits, familiarity and an uncaring attitude. This sets the stage for future
encounters with prospective family members.

There have been some landmark cases that have allowed a child to
divorce his or her parents, but most of them are *"stuck"* with the
relatives they're born with. Then, when they marry, they inherit all their
new spouse's relatives! If their marriage breaks up, these relatives will
likely remain part of their lives because of their children. Therefore, it's
so important to make that extra effort to get along with difficult
relatives and in-laws.

Couples who stay together *"because of the children"* are often
surprised by the reaction of their children when they finally decide to
separate. Their children wonder why their parents stayed together as
long as they did.

Because of the high divorce rate, one or more of their parents may end
up as stepparents with all its inherent problems. They may find that they
need *all* the skills identified in this book, to make a success of this
particularly difficult relationship.

### Angry Parents

Maybe it was over his leaving the toilet seat up, resulting in her taking
an unexpected skinny dip. Or maybe it was because she left her
pantyhose dangling on the shower rod like a team of high-wire walkers.
Or perhaps it was because they both never seem to have enough cold
cash to keep up with the Joneses. Different triggers - same result.

At some time during most relationships, couples argue and often the
dispute is only a symptom of an underlying issue. Arguments, for better
or worse, are how some people make contact. These spats can be played
out in other things, like money, sex and power - but the basic thing is
about closeness and distance. All fights are about what kind of
relationship they have and who's in control. They need to learn how to
fight fair. These signs often characterise such fights:

- Criticism. Instead of attacking the issue, the person aims for the other's weaknesses.
- Defensiveness. The person feels threatened, so shuts off his/her ears to what the other is saying.
- Contempt. The person views his/her partner in an extremely negative light, having no positive regard for him or her.
- Gives *"the Silent Treatment"*. A partner protects his/her ground by avoiding the other, walking out on discussions or changing the subject.

In any dispute, emotions steer things, making rational decisions difficult. Many fights start with tossing blame. Nothing keeps a person angrier than if another denigrates their character. It takes a lot of courage to stop and talk about what's happening under the surface of the argument - about the hidden motives behind the argument. Someone needs to ask, *'Why are we fighting? I can't take this.'* which makes the person vulnerable. It's as if they've laid down their weapon - but if the relationship is meaningful, it's worth it. If they keep seeing the other person as an enemy - it's difficult to move on and settle things.

Children, teens, young adults and adult children are more upset by non-verbal expressions of anger such as sarcasm and the silent treatment than originally thought. They hate it even more if it's their parents using weaponry of this kind to show anger and watch how their parents act after they fight. Unresolved anger bothers all children and they're very quick to pick up tension between their parents. Arguments that aren't resolved during the confrontation often sit there like time bombs and the children wait anxiously for them to erupt again.

Arguments that express anger in a physical way, that use hitting and pushing, are far more damaging and hard to forget. Children learn that hitting and pushing during arguments are acceptable behaviour. This is passed on to their playmates and friends and they wonder why they have problems getting along with others.

Arguments have their place. Those arguments that conclude with parents apologising to each other, negotiating and/or compromising and showing obvious signs that the argument is solved, help children understand that all arguments aren't wrong. This kind of argument doesn't have as lasting an effect on children and they learn that arguments are all right - if things are solved peacefully at the end with no winners and no losers.

### Disciplines in Public

'*As hard as I try to get along and do everything to please my parents, my Dad embarrasses me by disciplining me in public. This is especially embarrassing when he does it around my friends. Lately, I've hated to go out with him socially or have my friends over. How can I get him to realise how demoralising this is to me?*'

It depends on the background of your father and what his values and beliefs are. If he's willing to listen to you on other matters, find a time the two of you can be alone. Make sure he's in a receptive mood. Explain why you're reluctant to be out with him socially or to have your friends over and how you feel when he embarrasses you. State you could accept his criticism far better if he gave it privately. Then, ask if you can count on him to do this in the future.

If he's not receptive, talk to your mom and have her speak on your behalf. Possibly the three of you should have a discussion and resolve the problem using a trained family counsellor if necessary.

### Won't back me up

'*The other day, neighbours complained to my parents about something I supposedly did to damage their fence. My parents didn't even give me a chance to defend myself and bawled me out in front of the neighbour.*

'*I'm more hurt by my parent's reaction than the accusation. They let me down by not giving me a chance to defend myself. I haven't talked to them for three days; I'm so hurt about this. I'm reluctant to bring it up again, even though I can prove I was not the one who did the damage.*'

Bring it up again, give your proof and explain how you felt when they let you down. Air your feelings, but don't air them in an accusatory tone. Say, for instance, '*Mom and Dad, I want to talk to you about something that's been bothering me for three days. Will you promise to listen to me and try to understand what I'm saying?*'

When they give you their word they will listen, continue, '*The other day when Mr. Jones accused me of damaging his fence, you bawled me out for doing it. I was very hurt by your reaction, because you see; I was at school at that time teaching little children bicycle safety. You automatically assumed that I was guilty and that hurt me a lot. I'd like you to go with me while I talk to Mr. Jones. If necessary, I'll get Mike Martin from the school to accompany me as well. But I didn't damage his fence.*'

Your parents by this time should be convinced that you were innocent and get the message that you were very hurt by their refusal to hear you out. End the conversation with, *'In the future, will you promise to hear my side of the story before deciding?'*

### Miscarriage and pregnancy

*'I've been an only child all my life. I'm now fifteen and was upset when I learned that my mother was pregnant. The last thing I wanted around was a squalling baby. When my parents announced this to me, they were quite embarrassed. The pregnancy was unexpected, but not unwanted. They've started preparing, by getting all their baby things back from our relatives.*

*'By the time my mother was just four months pregnant, all three of us were very excited about having another baby in the family. Unfortunately, my mother had a miscarriage. She and my dad are so sad about it and I feel so guilty because I really didn't want the baby at first.'*

Between ten and thirty percent of all pregnancies end in miscarriage and the older the mother, the more likelihood that this will happen. About half of early miscarriages involve a missing or extra chromosome in the foetus. Heavy smoking or alcohol use can cause some miscarriages. Miscarriage is not likely to be caused by a fall or having sex.

Friends and family may be uncomfortable discussing the end of a short-lived pregnancy, but the effect on the woman is strong and may require a mourning period of three to twelve months. Tell her how sorry you are that she lost the baby. Listen to her – let her talk. Avoid advising, judging or interpreting. Avoid comments like: *'Keep your chin up.'* *'It's nature's way of getting rid of defective babies.'* Or *'That's life.'*

*'My mother has just announced that she's pregnant! She's 45 and far too old to have another baby!'*

Increasingly, women are bearing children at what was once considered an advanced age. In fact, births to women in their early 40s have increased by 50 per cent since 1970. For some, it's the story of *"the accident"* - women who have had their children, thought that pregnancy was behind them and then discovered they were pregnant. Many think they're going through early menopause, but those who'd had recent pregnancies knew their bodies well enough to go out and purchase a pregnancy test.

For others, it is a long-sought pregnancy after years of trying or at a chosen point in a woman's career. That's not to say that older pregnancies are immune to problems. Some have an enormous amount of morning sickness and some deliver early - a phenomenon not uncommon in older women and mothers carrying twins. It's common knowledge that the risk to the baby of Down's syndrome increases with age of the mother. Older women are also at higher risk of developing gestational diabetes as well as pregnancy-induced hypertension (toxaemia) that in its severest form can cause life-threatening seizures. But despite those risks, experts say, pregnancy in a healthy, fit woman over 40 should not be any different than in a younger woman except that she'll need more rest.

Your mother will need your support and help throughout her pregnancy - especially getting things done around the home. Be sure you're there when she needs you with your support and help.

### Allergies

*'I'm allergic to cats, but my parents have them. I can tolerate being in their home for short visits, but when their cat comes near me, I have a terrible time breathing. Is it proper for me to ask that they keep their pet in another room while I visit?'*

This is something you should discuss with them in detail **before** you decide to visit them. Explain your problem and ask for their co-operation. You're likely to be allergic to the cat's dandruff that would be throughout your parent's home. The only alternatives might be to have them visit you in your environment, meet them in a neutral place such as a restaurant or they get rid of the cat. Give them the alternatives and let them decide which one they wish to take.

### Uncommunicative Parents

*'My parents are always so uncommunicative with me and they don't converse very well with each other either. I can never get close to them, close enough that they relate their thoughts and feelings to me. I don't know how they feel about what I do, about the adult I've become; I need to guess. I'm finding that even when I ask them direct questions about items of importance to me - they hedge their answers. I realise they act this way with everyone and don't appear to need anyone except themselves. But this hurts me. What can I do to find out how they feel and think about me? I'm getting desperate in my attempts to get even a simple compliment on the things I do.'*

All children want and need the approval of their parents. In your parent's case, it's likely that neither of them has learned to look inside themselves to identify what's really happening to them and how they really feel about others. Many people, who have few close relationships with others, find they're often lonely and some feel deserted by others themselves, but don't know how to change the situation. They're afraid others will see what they're like inside - and this is often that they're afraid - afraid of what others think of them.

Open a conversation with your parents by using feedback. Describe how you feel shut out by them, can't get their approval and the terrible feelings you have of inadequacy. Tell them that you need them to be open and honest about how they feel about what you do and how you turned out as an adult.

Realize that this is their problem - don't make it yours. They too may need your nurturing (see section on Support groups, next).

To fulfil your need for acceptance, find the nurturing and acceptance you need from another caring parental figure. This can often be a close friend or relative of your family you've known since you were a child. Cultivate their friendship and let them help you gain the acceptance you need.

Although I didn't really need this kind of adult while I was growing up, I found that my parent's life-long friends became surrogate parents to me when my parents weren't available. When I was little, a common joke around my home was, that I would say to my mother (when she had refused a request), *'I'm going over to my "other mother's" place. She'll let me do this.'*

My mother would warn these *"other mothers"* (there were three of them - one an aunt) that I was on my way, so they knew what to expect. They never took sides, but just having someone neutral to listen to me, was often what got me through difficult situations. When my father died, and my mother had Alzheimer's disease, these *"other mothers"* were a great comfort to me and provided the mothering I still needed occasionally.

### Support Groups

If your parents have had a bad day and need someone to help them through it - who would they call? Everybody needs others to help him or her through the bad days and to celebrate good ones. The more support a person has the better but having two people on call is much better than having only one - because one person might be having a bad day themselves.

Even more effective are support groups that can help them deal with special problems such as alcoholism, drug, wife or child abuse, depression or severe emotional problems. Self-help groups are growing rapidly because they provide a unique service. The sense of belonging and acceptance that occurs when people have suffered something in common gives them the help they couldn't find elsewhere.

Your parents desperately need to set up a support group that will be there when they need them. You could be part of that support group. Right now, they're probably stranded on an island of their own, with little faith that others can help them. In the past, others may have let them down, so rather than rely on someone to help during bad times, they've learned to rough it out alone.

People of all ages need support groups. For many, the sudden death of a parent may make a person think for the first time about his or her own immortality. Strong friendship with other adults is necessary to replace the missing parental guidance they may have counted on up until that time.

### Parents throw my past at me

*'My parents are always throwing things I've done in the past at me. I'm tired of being reminded of my past indiscretions and actions.'*

Recognise when others are trying to manipulate you with this passive-aggressive behaviour by trying to make you feel guilty. The past can't be changed despite how you feel about things. Instead, if you identify things you did that you're not proud of, instead of wallowing in guilt, learn from the experience. If an apology is necessary to remove the guilt, then apologise.

When you feel you're being shoved around psychologically, state how you feel. The fact that others disapprove of things you do has nothing to do with what or who you are. You're not responsible for the happiness of others – they must make themselves happy. You're responsible for your emotions and they're responsible for theirs.

### Step-Parent

*'My mom is re-marrying and I'm going to be forced to share a room with my new step brother. I resent the fact that we're the ones who must*

*suffer because of this change. The rest of my siblings (new and old) are upset as well. How do we let our parents know that we resist this change in our lifestyle?'*

Here's how one family handled a similar trial:

*'We expected some skirmishes, but not a civil war when we remarried four years ago and combined eight teenagers. The kids liked each other, so being together all the time would only make life better - or so we thought. Instead, it was much worse. At first our problems focused on the house. It had made economic sense to live in my rambling old farmhouse in need of repairs instead of buying a new house - but that soon became a nightmare. My children resented doubling up to make room for three more children who got their rooms. My stepchildren missed their cosy suburban home surrounded by neighbours and public transportation. They disliked the fields and open country spaces that my children loved.*

*'When we told the children we planned to marry, we concentrated on what we considered the positives of financial security and having a full-time mother at home. But the only mother my children really wanted was their own.*

*'Children need time to adjust to remarriage and must be encouraged to discuss their concerns about the changes that will occur – instead of talking only about the "benefits". There's no such thing as an instant family. Stepfamilies that are thrown into things - instead of growing into them - may need time together before they begin to care about one another. Our children even objected to being called a family – insisting they were still two different entities. My stepchildren had a father in another state and I was trying to take his place. Liking me appeared to be a betrayal of him.*

*'Gradually, the children gave up the old and got on with the new. During this trying time, I needed - and got - lots of positive support from my wife. We made a lot of mistakes, but even while we were making them, we were slipping into a new family style a day at a time as we lived under the same roof. We fought a lot, laughed a little and gradually cared about each other's suffering. Today we laugh together about the things that used to make us cry.'*

So, you see - there is hope if everyone works together and they communicate both their good and bad feelings and work out compromises. You and your siblings (both old and new) will need to co-operate. However, don't expect your families to blend overnight.

### Dependent Mother

*'My father died three years ago, shortly after my marriage. Since that time, my mother has not been able to get on with her life and is constantly expecting her three married children to entertain and take care of her. She's only forty-seven and we feel she's far too dependent, but how do we help her through this?'*

It's difficult for women who lose a partner around whom they've built their lives. Men who lose their wives tend to re-partner much more quickly because they cannot bear to be on their own. Very few widows look for a new relationship unless they're very young when they become widowed. Widows have an additional social problem. Many are excluded from social functions because other women fear they will steal their husbands. Widows can be a threat at a dinner table in the same way as divorcees. The last thing these women probably want - is someone else's husband. Most just want their own husbands back.

Many widows feel extremely vulnerable. Many feel lost when their husbands die because he'd made all the big decisions or had chosen all the major purchases. Some remain closeted in their homes - frightened even at the prospect of facing others. Many of these women - because they are less likely to be the primary breadwinner - are more likely to be left financially vulnerable. For many, their husbands are dead - but not gone. They still dream about them, hold conversations in their minds with them and if they need to make a decision, they would try to imagine what their husbands would do.

Your mother probably depended fully on your father to make decisions for her and she was comfortable in that role. Suddenly, she now must make decisions for herself - possibly for the first time in her life. This can be overwhelming for her.

She believes that she should be dependent on others and must have someone stronger on whom to rely. While we all depend on others somewhat, there's no reason to encourage dependency, for it leads to loss of independence, individualism and self-expression. The dependent person is at the mercy of those who protect them. Dependency causes greater dependency. She fails to do things for herself or learn new skills and suffers from insecurity when her defenders are not available. She should strive for independence and responsibility and learn to refuse to

170

accept help just because others offer it. Taking risks - which could possibly result in failure - are worth trying. Failing is not a catastrophe.

Explain to her how she can make independent decisions by using the technique in Chapter 5 under *"Whiners and complainers"*. Encourage her to use the steps to make her own decisions without help and to socialise with her own peer group.

Will this be easy? No, it won't, but with the encouragement and support of you and your siblings (who must do the same) your mother can go from being dependent, to one who's getting on with her life.

***Fake Illnesses***

*'Whenever my mother has a conflict she complains that she has a migraine headache - especially now that she's going through menopause. Because of this, people tiptoe around her and try to keep her life stress-free. I'm beginning to think this is just an excuse not to discuss touchy subjects. How can I tell if her headaches are really real or just an excuse to manipulate us?'*

Seventy per cent of migraine patients are women, probably because fluxes in estrogen levels contribute to the nerve-cell disturbance. About a quarter of the migraines are stress-related. So, your mother is probably not faking it. Has she seen a doctor for treatment?

For the run-of-the-mill headache pain, over-the-counter drugs will normally keep discomfort in check. Migraines are trickier; it's important for her to learn how to spot one coming and have the right doctor-prescribed medication on hand. These people are warned of a pending migraine attack by hallucinatory auras, a pulsating (often one-sided headache) waves of nausea and the unbearable sensitivity to light, sound and smell. Whether episodes occur once a year or once a week - they usually last for the better part of a day, if not longer.

As any migraine sufferer knows, an attack can bring pain so intense that it obliterates work, family and thought. Yet for all the suffering it causes, the migraine is a mundane and commonplace ailment, afflicting about twelve per cent of the population. It's a trait passed along from parent to offspring. Seventy-five per cent of sufferers are thought to have an inherited predisposition to the disorder - so you or one of your siblings may also suffer from migraines, if not now, but likely in the future.

New forms of meditation, including biofeedback and self-hypnosis, as well as relaxation exercises, are mind-over-body ways to try to outsmart migraines. Scientists are testing a chelated form of magnesium supplements, as a possible migraine preventive. Unlike currently available magnesium pills (which can cause severe diarrhoea when taken in therapeutic doses) the new supplements are absorbed without being broken down and don't seem to have side effects. If your mother has migraines, she deserves sympathy – not antagonism.

### Stubborn Mother

*'My frail mother insists on walking seven blocks to and from her local store and then struggles back with her groceries. Her doctor has reprimanded her for this and insists she stop carrying heavy articles. I've suggested that she call me at work or I call her, three times a week so I can get a list of groceries she needs. I'll either pick them up on my way home from work and deliver them to her or pick her up and take her shopping. How do I get her to accept my help?'*

New ideas won't work unless you can get people to accept them. You might have to sell the new way. This is where planning comes in handy.

The following check list will help you cope with objections more effectively using this example situation.

Anticipate her perceived objections. If she said,

*'I don't want you to go out of your way for me. You have enough to do already, without helping me out.'* Your answer could be, *'I want you to let me do this for you, because I do have time to help you out. I'm afraid of having you overtaxing yourself and want you around for a long, long time.'*

Spoon-feed your idea or proposal gradually. Don't try to get immediate acceptance or compliance. The objection may be nothing more than a delaying tactic - the person's natural resistance to change.

*'I'd like you to think over an idea I had, that will help you do what your doctor says you should do. After I explain my idea to you, I'd like you to take a few days to see what you think of it. Here are the advantages I see of doing it this way... See if you can come up with any other solutions to this situation. I'll talk to you Monday about this.'*

Consider bringing up significant objections yourself instead of waiting for the other person to do it. *'I know you treasure your independence and don't like to rely on others, but I'd like you to give me the chance of helping you for a change.'*

Don't take the voiced objection for granted. People sometimes voice one complaint to mask another they would prefer to conceal. She objects by stating she likes the walk. She really dislikes having to rely on anyone else to help her. Collect irrefutable evidence so you can convince her that her objections are ill founded (if such is the case). *'I know you think I'm too busy, but I'm not. You were always there for me when I needed you and I'd like you to give me the chance of giving back to you for a change.'*

Anticipate and prepare for as many possible objections as you can. Develop a plan for handling each objection. *'As an alternative, one day a week, I'll pick you up and take you shopping. This will allow you to get out more.'*

Work out a practical way to eliminate the objection if you possibly can. *'I still expect you'll want to take walks, but you'll have the advantage that you can go in any direction you want - instead of only to the store to bring home heavy bags of groceries. You've told me you're worn out after shopping, just think how nice it will be to have your walk and come home refreshed.'*

If you're unable to eliminate problems, try to find a way to compensate. As a last resort, buy her light-weight grocery cart so she can pull rather than carry her parcels. Let her know that you expect her to call you when she needs larger supplies or make plans to take her for a big shop once a week anyway.

Rally enough benefits to win her support and co-operation despite the objection. *'You'll be healthier. You'll probably live longer. You won't get tired from shopping. You'll see me more often. You'll make me feel better because I can help you for a change.'*

### Alcoholism

*'I'm concerned about my mother. Now that she and my father have separated, I notice that she drinks much more alcohol than she used to. What is this likely to do to her?'*

Have a heart-to-heart talk with her outlining your concerns. Explain the following information about females and alcohol:

When it comes to drinking alcohol, the gender gap may be at its widest. According to researchers, men and women shouldn't be compared when looking at the health risks of alcoholic beverages. While men generally consume more alcohol than women, emerging research shows that women are suffering far greater consequences from drinking. This is especially true in the elderly.

Alcohol is metabolised differently in women and has a stronger impact on a woman's body than a man's. Among heavy drinkers - usually defined as fourteen or more drinks a week - alcohol causes physical ailments, such as liver disease, far quicker in women. Women have more body fat and less body water, allowing alcohol to move into the bloodstream faster. They also appear to have less of an enzyme called alcohol dehydrogenase, which metabolises alcohol in the stomach. Therefore, more alcohol is getting into the system and more is getting to the liver.

Some studies show that as few as three drinks a week may increase a woman's risk of breast cancer by fifty percent. Breast cancer is the second leading cause of cancer death among women. Alcohol may also make women more susceptible to hemorrhagic stroke in which blood vessels break. Alcohol may interfere with bone calcification, making women at higher risk for osteoporosis.

However other studies show that drinking moderate amounts of alcohol - particularly wine - can protect both sexes against heart disease. This is especially important for women because heart disease is the leading cause of death in women. Post-menopausal women who drink moderately are probably doing little harm and may be lowering their risk of heart disease.

Unfortunately, most women who acknowledge that they have an alcohol problem find that male-oriented treatment is not effective. Alcohol research about women drinkers has been given the short shrift and few centres have done independent studies to learn the specific treatment required to help women deal with their alcoholism.

### Adapting to New Equipment

*'My father lives alone but has a hearing problem. I want to have a hearing enhancer put on his telephone, but he objects. How can I convince him of the benefits?'*

When seniors are apprehensive about trying something new, and are afraid they might fail (i.e., using a new telephone device that will assist their diminished hearing) do the following:

Try to find a way to get around the objection or to minimise its adverse effect. *'Once you learn how to use this, you can hear everything that*

174

*people say, instead of having to guess half the time. The only instruction you have to remember is to turn down or remove your hearing aid when you answer the phone; otherwise it will make a squealing noise.'*

Find a way to ease the person's mind, to make it less risky to go with your idea despite the objection. *'When I get home, I'll call you a few times, so you can practice before you phone your friends.'*

### Additional Needs

*'My parents are getting on in years but are very independent in nature. My mother has arthritis and has a difficult time getting around. What can I do to help them both stay independent?'*

For millions of people, helping aging parents and relatives maintain an independent life is a daily concern. How do we make home-sweet-home a safe place? This can be as simple as rearranging the furniture or getting rid of area rugs that are slippery underfoot. Age-proofing is not the same as child-proofing. You childproof a house because a baby doesn't know what's safe and not safe. In elder-proofing a house, you change the physical environment, so they can continue to function.

The chief goal of safe-proofing is to prevent falls, which are especially dangerous for the elderly. Falls occur because the environment is not right for the person. Getting older sometimes means poor vision, poor balance and weakness in the legs. There may be side effects of medication, heart problems or loss of sensation in the legs and feet due to diabetes or alcohol. Many elderly people use alcohol to self-medicate their physical and emotional problems.

If their existing home is a two-story or if it has many steps - they may need to move to another more suitable home. If they won't move, make sure stairwells are well lit and have handrails. Discourage them from placing items that are to go to the upper level on the stairs. You might install a chair lift if there's room on the stairs to accommodate such an appliance. There are many devices that can be used, or adjustments made around the average home or apartment to make things easier for the disabled:

- A device that can open doors with a remote-control device.
- Tilt chairs for easy entry and exit.
- Ramps, instead of stairs.
- Larger labels on medications for easy identification of medicines.

- Smaller windows they can remove as required for cleaning.
- Kitchen counters and drawers that go up and down with a motorised mechanism. Falls often result from reaching for things on high shelves. Rearrange items in their cabinets so they are within easy reach. Encourage them to sit down while doing kitchen tasks.
- Overhead light fixtures that can be lowered to allow for easy changing of light bulbs without a person having to stand on a chair or climb a ladder.
- Bathrooms are dangerous places with all those metal fixtures and slippery tiled surfaces. Consider installing safety rails in the bathtub and shower and near the toilet area. If they have a shower stall, they should be encouraged to use that instead of the bathtub - because it's less likely to cause falls. If they really like the tub - install a bath bench they can sit on while in the tub.
- Use non-slip bath mat and replace any area rugs with either a non-skid kind or install indoor-outdoor carpeting that doesn't slip at all. Install raised/padded toilet seats if required.
- Non-slip floors that will remove the danger of broken hips (a real threat to many seniors). In the bedroom (and all other rooms) remove scatter rugs. Make sure furniture is placed for easy navigation. Don't string electrical cords across the floor. If they get up in the middle of the night, they should be able to get around the room without tripping over a chair or an electrical cord.
- Lights that turn on and off when a person claps their hands or touches the lamp.

Encourage the elderly to walk during daylight hours and look for sidewalk depressions to avoid tripping over curbs. If they have bi-focal or tri-focal glasses, they may have difficulty going up and down curbs. Discourage them from wearing floppy shoes or slippers because these can cause falls.

Sometimes it can be difficult to convince a parent that these modifications are required. Nobody likes to think s/he is losing the ability to do all the things s/he once took for granted. Making changes requires relatives to be respectful of their fears and emotions. Others will listen if their doctor tells them rather than a relative.

## Older Driver

*'My father is seventy-five and still drives his car. His eyesight is failing, but he insists that he can drive safely. I think he's dangerous, not only to himself and my mother, but to others on the road. What can I do to convince him that he shouldn't be driving?'*

The issue here is likely your father's fear that others will take away his independence. Removal of driving privileges, for those who've had this valuable independence, is comparable to putting them in jail. Recognise that he probably sees this as others trying to force him into a state of dependency and he doesn't feel he's ready for this. To lessen his frustration in having his independence curtailed, brainstorm with other family members to come up with solutions to the problem.

Here are some you might consider:

1. Convince him to let your mother drive until she too can no longer do so.
2. Get your parents a charge account with a taxi company and those who can help financially, pay a set sum into that account each month.
3. Arrange with others who *can* drive to be on call when they need a ride. Accomplish this by giving your parents I.O.U.s stating, *'This is good for one free car ride.'* In exchange, your parents could repay the favour by giving out I.O.U.s of their own stating, *'One free babysitting session.'* Or, *'One knit sweater for three rides.'* Or, *'One free bird house.'*
4. Investigate the handibus situation in your area. If your parents are handicapped, they might qualify for help.
5. Get together with the children of other seniors, so you can share driving seniors to special events or shopping. It's just as easy to drive one senior, as it is two or three. With two or three seniors involved, you would only have to drive them every second or third time they require a ride.
6. Contact your local senior's centre to see if they can suggest alternatives.

If your father still insists on driving, get your family doctor involved and as a last resort, ask the police to intervene. (Your father doesn't need to know you've reported him). They'll probably insist that he have an eye test.

There are some horror stories about older drivers who refuse to stop driving, even though they've gone far past the time when they should. For example, an 80-year-old driver who ran a stop sign on a country highway at 100 km/h hit a man's car. Even though the victim was wearing his seatbelt, his back was broken, his jaw was splintered, his collarbone was driven into his lungs and he had more than 100 cuts on his face and hands.

The elderly driver who'd hit him had caused six accidents the previous year. After spending four months in hospital, the 82-year-old was driving again and a year later killed an entire family - including three children. He too died in that accident.

Incompetent licensing laws and a stubborn old man caused those injuries and deaths. And the story doesn't stop there. All the proceeds from the 82-year-old's estate went towards the settlement of the insurance claims of his victims. So, you see - not only are elderly drivers a danger to themselves and others, but also, they stand to lose everything they've saved over a lifetime in insurance claims. Your father could leave your mother destitute. That fact might also make him realise what a chance he's taking by continuing to drive.

### '*After all I've done for you!*'

'*My parents are always trying to make me feel guilty about the things I do or don't do for them and the time I spend with them. They act as if I 'owe' them a huge slice of my life because of 'All they've done for me!' Do I really owe them that much?*'

Children do not "*owe*" their parents anything. If the parents did a good job of raising their children to be responsible adults, the children would give gladly of their time, effort and energy. They also must be aware, that young parents are often stretched to the limit by demands on their time. The grandparents might have considerable time on their hands, but lack understanding of how little time their own children have to share with them. Their grown children dole out their time in small doses while they're busy building their own family unit and caring for their own children.

Use feedback to describe how you feel about them trying to make you feel guilty. Say, '*Mom are you trying to make me feel guilty because I don't spend more time with you? If you are – I don't appreciate your doing this. I'm stretched to the limit as it is and don't need the added stress of feeling guilty about not spending more time with you. Could you please refrain from doing that in the future?*'

## Responsible for my failing parents

*'My parents' health is failing, and it's become my responsibility to oversee their care. How can I manage this extra responsibility along with my own family and job obligations?'*

Try to get your siblings to pitch in and help. If everyone shares the load - the load gets lighter.

Often those who are still in their forties (mainly women) and are still responsible for growing children, find they have the added responsibility for aging parents as well. This group might feel pulled at both ends by the needs of both their children and their parents. They may wonder when they'll have time to spend on activities for themselves. In other families, by the time the grandchildren have grown, the parents can spend more time, energy and effort on not only their own needs, but also those of their parents.

This change in roles - children looking after parents and parents becoming dependent on children - is a transition for all involved. Suddenly the parental support the grown children had expected to last a lifetime and had counted on has disappeared. Some feel as if life has cheated them and they feel adrift in life for the first time. They become the major decision-makers for the three generations in the family unit.

Studies show that nurturing parents who give because they want to give (not for what they expect back) will likely breed the same loving and caring attitude in their children. But children are individuals too. Some are very nurturing in nature - others aren't. Parents can't expect the same kind of caring from all their children. The old expression: *'What goes around, comes around,'* is often true in the care of senior parents.

Women do most of the looking-after of elderly parents regardless of whether they're their own parents or their spouses'. Most have full-time jobs and children of their own. As the demands increase, the part of their life that suffers most is their fun time with friends, their children and their spouses. It can also have a heavy financial toll if the woman must give up her full- or part-time job to become a parent's caregiver. Even when the burden of the hands-on care is over, and the parent is in a nursing home, she remains the parent's watchdog. She remains the defender of their rights and protector of their well-being.

For many caregivers, the only respite they may have, is taking their parents to adult day care centres or have Meals on Wheels provide some of their meals.

Fortunately, many companies have begun to explore the types of help they can offer to employees who must look after elderly parents. Some consider flexible work schedules or sabbatical leave for employees who need time off to care for elderly relatives.

Some caregivers of elderly parents find the pressures so intense that they're driven to abusive practices such as:

- Cheating them financially.
- Mistreating them emotionally or physically.
- Cutting them off from seeing their friends.

Caregivers must monitor their own actions and ask for professional help if the pressures on them cause any of the above serious complications. If caregivers find that they're close to doing these things, it's time to re-evaluate their situation and obtain help.

### Grumpy Dad

*'I knew in my heart that having my widowed father come to live with us a year ago wouldn't work out. This is because with non-family members, he always appears happy, but with his immediate family he's always been a difficult person to deal with.'*

From the beginning, she felt pulled four ways by the needs of her children, her husband, her job and the extra demands of her father, who expected her to wait on him hand and foot. Although he could help, the only contribution he made to the smooth-running of their home was a small portion of his pension check - never his time and effort. Why should he? He'd never lifted a hand to help around the home during his marriage - so why should he start now?

His daughter had talked to him often about his lack of co-operation, but he refused to listen. She needs to try one more time to explain how upset she is by his stubborn and un-cooperative attitude. Using Toughlove, she would explain exactly the help she expects him to give and the consequences (he'll have to live elsewhere) if his behaviour doesn't change.

### Everyone must Love Her

*'My mother turns herself inside out trying to please everyone. She loses sleep and gets very depressed if she thinks she's slighted anyone. How can I convince her that it's impossible to please everyone all the time?'*

180

Some people must have everyone – spouse, children, bosses, friends, shopkeepers and even the person who comes to the door selling magazines think they're the greatest. This is irrational because it's an unattainable goal. When your mother does this, she become less self-directing and more insecure. She truly does need to understand that she can't please all the people, all the time and be willing to live with that fact without feeling guilty.

When dealing with her, explain how impossible it is for her to please everyone. Help her understand that she shouldn't let others decide the kind of day she's going to have (see chapter 1). Encourage her to take control of her responses to negative situations and remind her that she can't blame others for her negative responses to their actions.

### *Always Phoning*

*'My mother calls me every night and I find myself on the phone for half an hour. This interferes with what my wife and I have planned for the evening. I hate to be rude to her, because I think I'm the only one she talks to all day.'*

I've found that when people don't have something to get up for every morning, they're lethargic and depend on others to amuse them and keep them company. Please help this woman channel her nurturing impulses in other directions by encouraging her to:

- Help an older neighbour who can't leave home to do her shopping.
- Introduce her to another single person who is lonely.
- Suggest that she visit seniors in a retirement home who have few visitors.
- Get a pet to keep her company and give her something to get up for every day.
- Give help to a young mother with two or three children who must take her children shopping.
- Help a young family who can't afford a babysitter to have some private social time for themselves.
- Get her involved in community club activities.
- Help a newly arrived citizen find his or her way around your monetary system, how to get around in our city, agencies that can help them adjust, courses to help them speak her language better.
- Have her join a seniors' group.

### No Will

*'My father refuses to make out a will. I'm worried about how my mother will manage if he doesn't. How can I convince him that it's necessary to have a will?'*

A will is the only legally recognised document that allows us to distribute all our estate to others after our death. If your father dies without a will, the government will determine the division and distribution of his estate according to local laws. They'll likely appoint an administrator who's not likely to be the one your father would select, if he had had the chance. Keep encouraging him, by pointing out the benefits of having a will.

If you can convince him to write a will, he needs to give careful thought to the choice of executor who's responsible for arranging, the payment of debts and distributing the estate according to his will.

If you haven't made out a will yourself, make it a priority item to tackle tomorrow.

### *Prostate Cancer*

*'My father died of prostate cancer twenty years ago and now that I'm getting close to sixty, I'm terrified that I'll get it too. What are some of the facts I need to know about the disease and how can I prevent it from happening to me?'*

Although fifty percent of men over forty have prostate problems – usually they're not cancer-related. Whether a benign enlargement of the gland, bacterial infection or cancer causes the problem, men should watch for the following symptoms:

- Frequent, difficult or painful urination;
- Dribbling urine;
- Blood or pus in the urine;
- Pain in the lower back, pelvic area or upper thighs; or
- Painful ejaculation.

Growths on the prostate can often be found before the man feels any symptoms. If the growth is cancerous, treatment can begin before it spreads. One in eleven men will get prostate cancer and one-third of those diagnosed will die from prostate cancer. Because your father had prostate cancer, you would be five to six times more likely to contract it, so you should have been having yearly prostate examinations after you turned forty.

All susceptible men are encouraged to have a regular prostate-specific-antigen (PSA) exam, which is a blood test that helps detect prostate tumours. If your level is higher than normal, it doesn't mean you have cancer, but it's a good sign that there's something wrong. A biopsy and bone scan are done to rule out cancer and diagnose the problem. With prostate cancer, there are a few choices, including surgery to remove the prostate or radiation treatment. Unfortunately, about one-third of all patients become impotent from the treatment.

### Won't see a doctor

He died of colon cancer at the age of 51, only five months after the diagnosis, but his family thinks he suffered for at least a decade. They knew something was wrong, but they also knew to keep their distance when *"stomach trouble"* made him quarrelsome. No one dared suggest he see a doctor, because he hadn't seen one since he was a teenager. Physicians agree that notably middle-aged men put themselves at serious risk of a catastrophic diagnosis and a shortened lifespan by failing to see a doctor regularly. Seized by fear and delusions of invincibility, they hide their ills from the world, causing their families tremendous emotional distress and their bodies unknown harm.

### Travel Dangers

*'My parents do a lot of travelling. Since September 11th, 2001 I've been afraid every time they leave home. What things can they do to keep safe when travelling?'*

Nothing is likely going to stop terrorists from committing their horrific acts, most of which are unpredictable. It's the luck of the draw for most people, whether they're chosen to be their victims. Therefore, because it's not within your parent's power to change the situation – so stop worrying about it! Here are some of the things your parents can do about those situations they *can* control while travelling:

- When travelling out of the country, make sure they have additional medical coverage. They should know their blood type in case of emergency.
- Put identification inside their bag as well as outside.
- While travelling on an airplane they should keep important documents, traveller's cheques and jewellery on their person or

183

with them in a carry-on bag, purse or briefcase. This might also include a few basic survival items - a toilet kit, a change of underwear, etc., in case their bags don't arrive when they do.

- Use their business card on their luggage tags. That way, if they're leaving the city, thieves won't be able to tell from looking at their luggage where their home is.

- Allow plenty of time for connecting flights. They might be able to make connections in twenty minutes, but their luggage isn't likely to (especially if they're changing planes).

- Have them check for damage on a rental car and make sure it's noted on the contract *before* they leave the lot.

- Check to see if their personal car-insurance company offers car-rental insurance.

- Don't rely solely on the hotel's wake-up call. Carry a small alarm clock of their own as backup.

- If they're arriving late at night, call their hotel and let them know they're on their way. Many have an airport pickup service.

- Book into hotels that are advertised as *"business"* hotels rather than *"tourist"* hotels. They're less likely to get screaming children running up and down the hallways.

- Make sure their hotel reservation is guaranteed with a payment or credit-card number for the first night. (A confirmed reservation that is not guaranteed will only be held until 6:00 pm.)

- If they're travelling on business, when checking in, let the hotel know they're there on business. Give them a business card. Most hotels have corporate rates.

- If the registration clerk announces within earshot of others, the number of their room or gives them directions on how to find it, they should tell the clerk they'd like another room and explain why.

- When they're settled in their room, determine where the fire escapes are (identify at least two outlets, so they have alternatives). Count the number of rooms from their suite to the fire escapes and whether they are to the left or right of their room. (If a fire were to occur, they might not be able to see the exit and might have to crawl along the floor and count rooms to get there.) Open the exit door to make sure it isn't locked. Determine whether it's an outside escape or part of the building itself.

- Look out their room window to notice the height of their room and the nature of their surroundings. Notice whether and how windows

184

open: do they slide right to left, left to right or straight up – or don't they open at all? Is there a balcony?

- When they retire at night, place their room key on the bedside table within easy reach. If a fire should occur, take the key with them when they leave the room. They may have to return to their room if the smoke is too heavy or if the fire is too close to their room. If they don't have their key, they may be stranded in a hallway that's an inferno.
- If they have noisy neighbours, complain to the front desk. If they're not satisfied with how they handle this, complain directly to the manager.
- If a late checkout is required, notify the front desk. The bellhop can keep their luggage in a storage room.

Here are some travelling tips for your mother when she travels alone:

- She shouldn't feel that she must eat in her room if she's alone. Encourage her to have a leisurely meal in the dining room and enjoy herself!
- When dining, she should expect a decent table where she has some privacy. She shouldn't accept a table next to a swinging kitchen door!
- Her bartender or server should not pass a note to her or serve her an unrequested drink without discussing the situation with her first. If she wishes to be alone, she should tell the bartender.
- She deserves respect. If she's addressed as *"sweetie"* or *"honey"* - she should discuss it with the manager.
- When she travels on business with a male colleague, she shouldn't meet in his hotel room or invite people to her room for a drink. This eliminates the risk of having to cope with unwanted advances.
- When the only place she has for a business meeting is her own hotel room, she should ask the hotel to arrange a suite.
- If her room doesn't appear suitable for a meeting, she could try a quiet corner of a restaurant.
- If she's entertaining guests at a restaurant, she should make it clear to the server (or when she's making the reservation) that the bill is to be charged to her room. It's hard for waiters and waitresses to know whom to bill if there are three or four people at the table.

## Divorce

*'My parents have been married for thirty years but have just announced that they're divorcing. My sister and I are devastated. How could this*

*happen after thirty years of marriage? They're in their fifties and I can't understand why they would do this at this late stage of their lives.'*

I can almost guarantee that the last child has left the nest and they have looked at their relationship and found it wanting. Sometimes couples just drift apart and continue together *"because of the children"*. It's possible that this is what's happened to your parents. It's possible that they don't have the same shared attitudes and values they had when they were first married. One might have defined differences of opinions to the other that they have kept suppressed to *"keep the peace"* in their marriage. They may have thought these important differences would go away with time, but they seldom do.

It's possible that the friendship they had with each other - the shared things they used to do together may not have happened for many years. Instead, they've focused their attention on you, their children, but are now in the position where they can think of themselves first. Maybe they are asking themselves *'Is this all there is?'*

They may have let themselves fall into the habit of *"sniping"* at each other or one may have the habit of giving gender put-downs to the other. They may not fight fair. If this happens often enough, the friendship between them may have made them rivals - rather than friends.

Your mother may be seeking intimacy and your father doesn't know how to provide it. Possibly she's looking for it in another man or another relationship. Possibly the fire has gone out in the passion department and they're both looking for it in others.

Or habits they tolerated earlier may over time have become unbearable. Your father's snoring might now be enough of a disturbance that it grates on your mother's nerves every night. Or your father may be tired of what he perceives as your mother nagging at him.

Your mother may be tired of the inequality in her marriage and your father may be tired of hearing her complain that he doesn't do his share around the house. Maybe your mother has told her *"girlfriends"* about her problems with your father and he found out.

Whatever the reason, they have likely thought long and hard before deciding to separate. It's your responsibility to be there and support them during this time of crisis. Don't take sides and don't let them place you in the middle. Refuse to discuss the other parent's faults – just give support.

# CHAPTER 8

# DIFFICULT IN-LAWS

## *Critical Mother-In-Law*

Mildred had problems with her interfering mother-in-law, Doris. Every Sunday, Mildred and her husband, Victor went to her in-laws for dinner. Because they both worked, they often had to play catch-up on the chores around the house Saturday. This left only Sunday for them to enjoy each other's company. Mildred objected to spending her only day off with her in-laws every week.

There was another more hidden reason behind her objections. She admitted that Doris was constantly giving her advice on how to iron shirts, bake, cook and keep house. She was also very critical of everything else Mildred seemed to do. Mildred finally spoke to Victor and explained her frustrations to him. She wrote down all the advice and criticism his mother had given her that past Sunday. He agreed that she had good reason for being upset and asked what she thought they could do about it. After much discussion, they decided that Mildred should try feedback. Mildred would let Doris know how her negative actions were affecting her and Victor would back her up if necessary.

Mildred decided to speak privately to Doris one evening. As tactfully as possible, she explained exactly what was happening and asked Doris's co-operation in overcoming the problems. It upset Doris to know that her well-intentioned advice had been taken so negatively. Mildred learned there had been no malice or one-upsmanship intended in Doris's advice-giving - that she merely wanted to help her daughter-in-law learn from her experience. Doris explained that she had no daughters of her own and had looked forward to the day when she could help her son's wives with domestic problems. After a serious heart-to-heart talk, they came up with the following solutions:

1.  They would change the Sunday visit to Tuesday evening for their weekly dinner and get-together.
2.  Whenever Mildred felt Doris was interfering or criticising her, she would hold up her hand giving a stop gesture. Doris agreed that this would be the signal she would watch for and would stop her criticism.

Mildred also realised that Doris had considerable knowledge of arts and crafts. She decided to ask her advice in areas where she felt she needed help. This eased the transition for Doris, who might otherwise have felt rejected. Each woman learned to be more tolerant of the wishes, desire and aspirations of the other. Doris was far less critical and more helpful. Mildred came to depend on the tips on arts and crafts that Doris was gladly willing to give.

### Disciplines MY Children

*'When I visit my mother-in-law, she's always disciplining my children. I object to this. As I see it, I have two choices: I won't take my children there in the future or I'll explain to her how much I object to her actions. Are there any other options open to me?'*

First, ask yourself whether **you** should have been disciplining your children for what they were doing. If they needed guidance and you didn't provide it, your mother-in-law had every right to chastise your children while they were in her home. This is especially true if your children were being destructive to her belongings or rowdy with her pet.

If this was not the case, find examples of situations where she has disciplined your children and question her about why she felt the need to do this. Is she a parent who believes children should be seen and not heard? If it's traumatic for her to be around active children, leave them at home. Keep in mind that in this instance, it's **her** problem, not your children's and you should act accordingly.

### Loss of Love

*'My mother-in-law accuses me of "stealing her son" from her and that I don't let him spend enough time with her. He's spread so thin now with business and home responsibilities that he simply can't give her any more time. He feels very guilty when she pouts and complains to him. I know you'll suggest that my husband speak to her, but he says he can't do that. How can I deal with this ongoing problem?'*

Your husband should straighten his backbone and talk to her himself. He should explain that you haven't *"stolen"* him from her, that you're taking your correct place at his side as his full-time partner.

He could add, *'When you complain about the time I spend with you, I feel stretched like an elastic band. That elastic has been stretched as far as it can go. I have obligations to others both at work and at home that I must meet. This has no bearing on the time I spend with you. I have lots of love to go around and each love is different. For instance, I have love for you, love for my wife, love for my brothers and sisters, love for my children and love for my friends. One does not overshadow the other and are all important to me.'* You might have to speak on his behalf using similar words to these.

Either you or he should consider giving his mother an itinerary of what he does every day (including driving Jimmy to hockey, Susie to Brownies) and how difficult it is to spend more time with her. Then he should spend time to find activities that will keep her occupied. It sounds as if she's channelling all her energies towards her grown children. This could be the real challenge and both you and your husband should attack this problem, which should ultimately solve the initial one you mentioned.

### Unsupportive Brother-In-Law

*'I'm getting more and more furious at the way my brother-in-law is treating my sister. She worked for five years at a job she hated to support them while her husband was going to school. He's now working but won't do the same thing for her, so she can get into a job she likes.'*

Despite the enormous changes in the past two decades in gender roles, women continue to be the cheerleaders in our society. It's a supportive role; a *"stand by your man"* role that supports his career, his leisure activities and his personal pursuits. Often, however, the level of support is not reciprocated. A woman may get good at something and in doing so she leaves her husband behind. He may be good at something else but may be unaccustomed to having his wife be an expert at something he isn't. In a sense, he's being upstaged by her and becomes absorbed with other things. This means she's not being absorbed in the spouse. This power imbalance - and that's what it is - may be hard to think of as an abuse of power, but it is.

Women tend to be very supportive of men and whatever goals they're pursuing but the men tend to be less so - particularly if it's outside the domestic realm. If these women try to do anything (other than raise kids and cook meals) it doesn't get much support. It seems to be a threat to some men if women are trying to enlarge or change their role from the traditional one. While women's work enhances the family income, this can represent threats for men. The same is true for non-traditional leisure pursuits such as marathon running or skydiving or bungee jumping. The man may resent the woman pursuing these goals that he feels either competes with him or takes away from what he's expecting from the relationship. Or the woman feels resentful that she isn't getting the support that she feels she's entitled to that she's given freely to him in the pursuit of his goals.

Frequently one of the complaints these couples have is that their sexual relationship has gone down the tube. She may explain that she isn't interested in sex the way she used to be, but this can be a very effective but subtle way for her to retaliate for his lack of support. This means she's not being absorbed in the spouse.

Let your sister know that you support her and give her this information upon which to base the defence of her wishes to expand her knowledge and that it's not fair that her husband not take his turn in supporting her. He should account for why it was all right for her to work while he went to school – but not fair for her to expect the same from him. She may have to give consequences if he doesn't support her and she should be ready to deal with his response either positive or negative to her wishes to obtain more education.

### *Burned Out*

*'My father-in-law works so hard and most of the time he collapses as soon as he arrives home from work. He's nearing retirement and I'm afraid if he doesn't slow down he'll have a heart attack. He explains that he must work as hard as he can before he retires otherwise he won't have enough in his retirement fund. Both my husband and I are seriously worried about his health.'*

It sounds as if he's in the early stages of burnout. The description *"burnout"* is a good one, because it graphically conveys what happens when human organisms operate too fast and too long without proper fuel and lubrication. Sooner or later, the friction builds to such a degree, that parts begin to erode, crack or explode.

In the early stages of burnout (a battering form of depression that can cost people their jobs and ruin their health) sufferers may become irritable, procrastinate, miss deadlines, balk at routine assignments or accept challenging ones without properly preparing to handle them. They may suffer from insomnia, have eating problems, complain of ulcers, migraine or tension headaches and feel jumpy, hyperactive or lethargic. In the later stages, these symptoms become more severe and could lead to serious depression.

Some burnt-out cases tough it out, by resigning themselves to miserable lives, stoically accepting hypertension, ulcers, alcoholism, irritable bowels and other physical unpleasantness associated with stress. It's the price they pay for *"success"* or at least for maintaining their existing condition. Left untreated - burnout can be completely incapacitating and often requires hospitalisation.

He may be headed for burnout if he:

- Needs more hours to do less work;
- Suffers chronic fatigue;
- Has trouble eating and sleeping properly;
- Feels tired all the time;
- Feels down or depressed all the time;
- Is too busy to do routine things like phoning friends;
- Starts forgetting appointments and losing personal possessions, such as house keys;
- Feels he has no control over his life and his future seems as bleak as the present;
- Drinks more alcohol and uses more drugs, prescription and otherwise;
- Feels more and more irritable, cynical or disenchanted;
- Feels no real joy in anything, not even his job;
- Work is his life;
- Has the feeling he's failed, no matter how much he tries;
- Sees no hope for improvement;
- Is constantly complaining;
- Feels that no one cares;
- Withdraws from society;
- Feels upset, frustrated, angry most of the time;
- Feels intense job pressures;
- Is highly competitive in everything he does;
- Feels that no matter what he does - it won't be enough; and/or
- Fears that he's going under any day now.

Those who suffer from burnout often feel too tired to get out of bed. Even if they could muster the motivation, they're so cynical about their work that they wonder what it's all for. Their fatigue increases when they do get out of bed. Pretending they can cope only carries them so far. Instead of elevating their blood pressure, they should change their behaviour to see if they're making their day harder on themselves.

191

The final extreme of burnout can be suicide. In adults, one of the signs is that they get their life *"in order"*. They make sure their insurance is paid up, that their bills are paid, and their affairs are in order. Troubled children and teenagers may begin to give away their prized possessions to friends and relatives.

Observers of burnt-out people should be alert for signs of pending suicide attempts and step in to assist the person. Often a shoulder to cry on or an ear to bend is all that might be necessary. However, some may react to your attempts to help with hostility. Remain supportive and use facts to back up your belief that the person is in trouble.

Burnout sufferers who know they're in trouble should take a break from the pressure and allow themselves a time out before making major decisions. They need to get enough sleep and ensure they're eating and exercising properly. Participating in activities that bring them pleasure can get them through a bad day.

Denying how badly your father-in-law feels, with the hope that the problem will disappear, won't solve his burnout. Sometimes the best remedy for burnout is to confide in others - family members, co-workers or friends. Offer your help by discussing your concerns about him. If he has serious difficulty overcoming his burnout, he should consider seeking professional help before it defeats him, ruins his quality of life or cause serious health problems.

### Road Rage

*'My father-in-law drives like a maniac. He blows up when he's behind other drivers when they; drive slower than the speed limit, tailgate him, use cordless phones, pull out of a side-street in front of him or don't bother to signal before changing lanes. His middle finger is in a constant state of red alert and he spends most of his time on the road cussing just about everyone who comes close to him.'*

He's suffering from chronic road rage that's a growing problem everywhere. People have died in disputes between drivers and police say reports of incidents where one driver has got out of the vehicle and confronted another are daily occurrences. Many are likely to honk their horn or shake their fist, but there's no doubt people get angry when they think their space has been violated.

So why does he lose his cool? Are other drivers really that bad or does the mild-mannered accountant turn into a monster when he gets behind the wheel? Many people change personalities when they get into a car. When they're in a car, they're in a suit of armour and feel much more empowered. Cars and guns are very similar. If you are inclined to be aggressive and you have a gun in your hand; then you feel powerful. The same thing happens when we get into a car. However, a lot of things are out of your control when you're driving and combine that with the added feelings of power and you've got road rage looking for a place to happen. If they have a near-miss with another car - they're invading your space - so you honk your horn at them.

There are far more collisions in the winter and commuting hours are the most dangerous. Not too many people are in a hurry to get to work. The afternoon commute is the real nerve jangler. That's because people are more likely to be stressed and tired after work. They're also more likely to be in a hurry to get home to some peace and quiet. Monday and Tuesday are the most accident-free days.

Here are other road rage stories:

A woman honked her horn at a man who nosed in front of her at a construction site. Just down the road, he stopped and got out of his vehicle. They argued, and the man ended up pouring his coffee over the hood of her car before storming off.

Two men confronted each other at an intersection and argued loudly before one man climbed right over the car to get at the other man, who ran off.

One woman when driving to work was cut off by a small truck. She slammed on the brakes, which forced her body over the steering wheel causing the horn to honk loudly. At the next intersection, the truck driver got out of his truck. She locked her doors. He came back to her window and shouted, *'Do you have a problem?'* The woman (dressed in a very business-like suit) diffused the situation by calmly asking, *'You didn't get it last night, did you?'* The man gave a startled response, threw his hands in the air and returned to his truck. The woman observed him explaining what she had said to two other men in the truck (he had been showing off). When the two other men looked back, she smiled and waved to them diffusing the situation even further.

When a man gave the finger to one woman along with several verbal expletives, she responded, *'Hi! Tell your mother hello for me!'* The look on the man's face gave her a chuckle, her blood pressure didn't go up and the clod likely thought before he yelled at someone the next time.

193

I remember one day when I came abreast of a man on a motorcycle wearing a Hell's Angel's leather jacket. I was old enough to be his grandmother. I smiled, rolled down my window and asked, *'Does your mother know you're not wearing your helmet?'* He smiled sheepishly, took his helmet off its stand behind him and put it on. We both chuckled over the incident.

If people have had a bad day at work or at home, they should not drive. People who bring their emotions to the road - get into accidents.

When held up in rush-hour traffic and must sit and fume for five minutes – all their aggressive emotions surface. If they're wise they'll force themselves to calm down and settle back into a rational frame of mind. If they're unwise, they'll get in an accident that injures themselves and others - or worse.

And some allow the feelings of rage to linger once they get to their destinations and they continue to pass on their aggressiveness. Anyone who crosses their path suffers the consequences.

So, what helps? Driver education is one of the keys to reducing road rage by encouraging people to treat each other with dignity and respect and learning to share the road. They can't believe that this is my lane, my road and my set of lights. And everyone agrees that drivers need to start being less selfish. They need to look in the mirror and admit they have a problem.

So how should your father-in-law stop his road rage?

1.  Don't commute. This may sound obvious, but most people don't consider it. He should take public transportation, work a flexible schedule to avoid peak congestion times, get a job that lets him walk to work or work at home.
2.  Do whatever he can to create a relaxing environment in his car. Get the most comfortable car he can afford and equip it with a good set of listening resources.
3.  Work on reducing his overall stress level and prepare himself for the drive. He should expect something to go wrong and get relaxed before he gets into his car. Special breathing exercises that put him into more of an alpha or right-brained state, will relax him.
4.  Talking out loud to himself as he drives is a good way to avoid road rage. *'I will not lose my temper. I will not lose my temper.'* The brain processes the spoken word differently than thoughts. Telling himself verbally to calm down, to relax and breathe slower is more effective than just thinking it.

Until, and unless this happens, I would suggest you do not let him drive with you in the car.

### Smokers

'*My sister-in-law is a heavy smoker. I've never been able to spend much time in her home because I'm terribly allergic to cigarette smoke. When she comes to my home, she must smoke outside.*

'*Eighteen months ago, she mentioned that she and my brother were hoping she'd get pregnant. I asked her when she was going to stop smoking. She replied that she would do so when she knew she was pregnant. I explained that it would be too late by then; because the smoke would already have affected the foetus by the time she confirmed she was pregnant. I encouraged her to stop smoking right away so her baby wouldn't be affected.*

'*Last year she announced she was pregnant - and you guessed it - she smoked throughout her pregnancy. I let my brother know that I was furious about this. I couldn't stand being around her knowing what she was doing to their unborn child. When her daughter was born, she had a port-wine stain on her cheek that stood out about a quarter of an inch from her face (she still has it). Every time I see that poor little girl's face I picture a lit cigarette.*

'*I still cringe when I see my niece and get mad at her mother all over again. Her mother's still smoking heavily and doesn't even go outside to do so – so her daughter is exposed to her second-hand smoke. I wish there were some laws that prevented parents from doing this!*'

It still amazes me when I see a young woman smoking, whether she is pregnant or not. How anyone would want to smell like that and start a habit that would be so hard to stop and detrimental to those around them astounds me. Not only does smoking cause lung cancer and hundreds of other difficulties for the smoker and whoever is around them, but smokers will likely age much faster. I can always tell a smoker by their faces, their smoker's coughs and their voices (women's voices are huskier than normal).

The distinctive characteristics of smoker's face (which makes people look far older than their years) are present in 46 per cent of current smokers and 8 per cent in former smokers. Hopefully the threat of wrinkles may be a more powerful motivator to help your sister-in-law stop smoking, than the deadlier consequences, of lung cancer. Smoking depletes the skin's oxygen supply by reducing circulation. It decreases the formation of collagen, the skin's main structural component and may reduce the water content of the skin, all of which increase wrinkling.

She may think that having a face-lift will remedy things, but smokers have more complications and skin sloughing after face-lifts.

Speak to your brother and his wife and let them know how you feel about the dangerous environment they're forcing their daughter to live in. It's a shame that there isn't more protection for family members when there's a smoker in the home. Lobbying your lawmakers might be one way to make sure this destructive habit isn't allowed to affect vulnerable and unprotected children.

### *Wants more Grandchildren*

*'My mother-in-law has been badgering my husband and me to have another child. We have a busy three-year-old that keeps me hopping and we're simply not ready to have another child. However, even though we have told her to butt out - she keeps making inferences to the fact that he's an only child and needs someone to play with. We live on a prosperous farm and he doesn't regularly play with other children - but he does go to playschool twice a week and occasionally one of the mothers brings her children over to play with him. How should I deal with this pushy mother-in-law?'*

There's a snippy saying that states, *'What is it about No that you don't understand?'* That's what you probably feel like saying to her. However, that might just cause more tension between you. Your husband is the one who should speak to her using feedback, *'Mom, I know you mean well, but when you badger us about having another child we both get annoyed. Would you please not do so in the future?'*

**a) Describe the problem or situation.**
   *'When you badger us about having another child...'*
**b) Define what feelings or reactions.**
   *'We both get annoyed.'*
**c) Suggest a solution or ask them to provide a solution.**
   *'Would you please not do so in the future?'*

If necessary, he would go through the feedback steps to reinforce that he meant what he said. He'd need to be ready with the consequences if she continued doing what she's doing. He also might enlist his father to step in and chastise his mother for her behaviour.

196

### Former Brother-In-Law

*'When my sister and her husband Dick divorced, I continued to associate with her husband. He has now re-married and is living in another city. When I visit that city I often stay with Dick and his new family. My sister gets furious when she hears about this and accuses me of not being loyal to her. I enjoy staying with Dick and his family and have told her so.'*

There are many kinds of love and friendship. Just because he's your former brother-in-law doesn't mean that you must sever ties with him. Your sister must have a very low self-esteem level or is still hurting from the divorce. It's often the one who has been *"left"* that still feels this way (often for years) when a couple break up. I would guess that she was the one who was left and is still smarting emotionally from it. Talk to her about this, showing that you understand how she may still be feeling rejected by him, that you're sorry their break-up happened that way, but that it has nothing to do with your friendship with Dick and his new family.

### Can't see Grandchildren

*'My son and his wife separated, and she has custody of the children. She's moved away from where we live, and we never see them any more. We love our grandchildren and have been sending gifts for birthdays and Christmas, but never get an acknowledgement from them that they receive them. Should I keep on sending them gifts and how can we see them occasionally?'*

Your son must have times when he can see his children. Ask him if you could visit with them when he sees them. If he must travel to their location – ask if it would be all right if you went along with him during his next visit. Have him check out for you whether the children received your gifts or better yet - have him take the gifts when he visits his children.

You could also write a letter to your former daughter-in-law and ask specifically if you can see your grandchildren and when. If she refuses, ask why she's done so and be prepared for her answer. You might check with a lawyer to see whether you have any rights as the grandparents of these children to see them. The laws are changing, and you might be able to establish a regular visiting time with them. It's worth a try.

### Christmas Blues

*'My mother-in-law goes into a deep depression around Christmas, because her husband died two days after Christmas. How can we help her through this terrible time?'*

There are three important reasons why it's important to recognise and treat severe depression.

- First, thoughts of suicide are extremely common – some even carry out their thoughts. Depression can be anger turned against themselves because they feel helpless or unable to change the situation.
- Second, people with depression suffer. Their quality of life is poor and they're unable to be enthusiastic or enjoy activities. Prompt treatment makes most people feel better.
- Third, identifying depression often can clarify what's wrong with the person who complains about an unending series of physical complaints. This can be a big relief to the person's physician, who can then save the patient the expense and risk of diagnostic tests if it's known that the person is suffering from depression.

How can she keep from becoming depressed? One of the cures may be to increase her level of activity. Get her involved in your family holiday preparations - baking, wrapping gifts - having get-togethers with friends. This means that she won't have time to sit in front of the television set or stare out the window mulling over her loneliness.

Here are more steps she can take by herself to ward off the *"holiday blues"*:

- Encourage her to spend time with her friends if you or other family members aren't available.
- Have her ask other lonely or despondent people over for a fun-filled holiday get-together.
- Do something special for someone else every day (it's the little things that count).
- Get enough physical exercise - (but have her check with her doctor before beginning any new strenuous activity).
- Listen to music or read a good book.
- Laugh - instead of watching a dreary movie or television program, watch a comedy where she can laugh to relieve her tensions. Letting the *"little kid"* in her have fun, is a pleasant way to get her feet back on the ground during trying times.
- Get away from it all - take a nature walk.
- Join a support group - don't go it alone.
- Use positive, not negative thinking.

- Get the proper amount of sleep and rest, but don't use sleep as an escape from her problems.
- Have someone give her a soothing massage that can do wonders to raise her physical well-being.

### *Moving Away*

*'My mother and father-in-law have lived in their home for over thirty years, but it's become too much for them to look after so they've decided to move into an apartment. They live in another city to us and want to stay there with their friends. However, they're worried about moving to a new place and especially about having new neighbours. They had wonderful neighbours who were very helpful when they were ill and looked after their home when they were away. What kind of things can I suggest they do after they get settled in their new home?'*

Friends and relatives may take a while to reach them in an emergency. Suggest they keep the following points in mind when dealing with their new neighbours. A friendly and positive neighbour can enhance the sense of security and well-being, while a hostile and negative neighbour can be a source of stress, emotional turbulence, anger, irritation, jealousy and criticism. Much of our laughter and happiness depends upon the relationship we have with people around us such as our friends, relatives and especially our neighbours. Our neighbours can play an important role in the well-being of any family because they're available twenty-four hours a day and live next door.

Help your parents start off on the right foot by remembering that they will likely need their neighbour's help:

- During an emergency - fire, mishap, theft, robbery, gas leakage (especially if your parents are away or on holidays) or should your parent's have a medical emergency or death in the family.
- Looking after your parents' home, pets, plants and mail while they're away for a few hours or days (a mutual understanding).
- Looking after their important letters and documents when they're away for a long time.
- Sharing their successes and achievements and giving moral support during crisis and bereavement.

They can build rapport with their neighbours by:

- Expressing gratitude - even if they do a small favour.

- Being ready to help their neighbour in the same manner (which is like insurance for your parents to gain their neighbour's help and support when it's required).
- Remembering their neighbour's birthdays (especially their children's) their wedding anniversaries and by congratulating them personally or sending flowers or greeting cards.
- Periodically sending small gifts to make their neighbours feel special.
- Paying authentic compliments about their house, children, their successes and achievements.
- Delivering letters and documents promptly when incorrectly delivered to their address.
- Not playing loud music during parties and celebrations. They should ask their neighbours to their events - then they aren't likely to complain.
- Avoiding litter in a common passage or open places that might cause inconvenience to their neighbours.
- Careful and compassionate when handling fights amongst children.

# CONCLUSION

### *Are you ready for your difficult siblings, relatives and In-Laws?*

You've been given the tools that can empower you to deal with irate, rude, impatient, emotional, upset, persistent and aggressive relatives and in-laws. These crucial people skills permit you to deal with all types of difficult people and circumstances. Learn these skills and you can't help but enhance your relationships with your siblings, relatives and in-laws.

Your proficiency in people skills will help you control your moods and keep you cool under fire. You'll start on the road to understanding why men and women have such an arduous time communicating with each other and why they're likely to interpret situations differently. If you practice the techniques, you'll be able to:

- Master your mood swings by maintaining control when faced with negative situations;
- Raise your self-esteem level because you're in control of your emotions;
- Keep your cool under fire;
- Stop wasting your precious energy on negative emotions;
- Turn off hurt, guilty or defensive feelings;
- Give and receive criticism with more confidence;
- Know how male and female communication styles differ;
- Know what kind of person you are and how to get along with other personality types;
- Understand passive, aggressive, assertive, passive resistant, indirect aggressive and passive-aggressive behaviours;
- Comprehend the importance of non-verbal communication;
- Use various communication skills such as paraphrasing, feedback, listening and speaking;
- Identify manipulative behaviour and know how to deal with it in a forthright manner;
- Deal with whiners, bellyachers and complainers;
- Detect and deal with anger in yourself and others; and
- Deal with difficult siblings, relatives, seniors and in-laws.

Learn the techniques and practice them daily. They <u>do</u> work! But like any new skill, you'll have to use them unfailingly until they become spontaneous. If you do, you can look forward to being able to control how you deal with and react to others.

No longer will you allow others to decide what kind of day you have. Because you've gained this control, your self-esteem level will raise accordingly. The more self-assured you are, the less stress and apprehension you'll feel, which will give you more stamina and enthusiasm. Use these skills and brace yourself for the improved communication that will inevitably follow.

# Appendix A
## UNIQUE CAREER COUNSELLING SERVICE

Available via e-mail

Provided by Roberta Cava of:
Cava Consulting,
info@dealingwithdifficultpeople.info

In these hard, economic times, are you finding it difficult to find suitable employment in your field of work? How would you like to expand those opportunities? This unique career counselling service will enable you to determine your transferrable skills and identify another 20 to 40 occupations where you could use those skills.

An investment of **$175.00** (AUD) will provide you with an extensive report that includes:

- A list of your transferrable skills
- 20 to 40 primary and secondary occupations you could investigate that use your transferrable skills
- A psychological report that includes:

1. Your strengths in the areas of interest, ability, values, personality, capacity
2. Interest, ability and personality profiles
3. What you think your skills are compared to what they really are
4. Determine your management, persuasive, social artistic, clerical, mechanical, investigative and operational abilities
5. Whether you are outgoing, reserved, factual, creative, analytical, caring organised or causal
6. Your ability to think, reason and solve problems
7. Values inventory
8. Your stamina level
9. Your I.Q. Score
10. Performance and personality characteristics
11. Motivational and De-motivational factors
12. Whether you have what it takes to become an entrepreneur and have your own business

To learn more, go to our web page and follow the prompts:

www.dealingwithdifficultpeople.info/unique-career-counselling-service

For more information, contact Roberta Cava at:

info@dealingwithdifficultpeople.info

# BIBLIOGRAPHY

Cava, Roberta, *Dealing with Difficult People; How to deal with nasty customers, demanding bosses and uncooperative colleagues* (22 publishers in 16 languages)

Cava, Roberta, *Dealing with Difficult Spouses and Children; How to handle difficult family problems,* Cava Consulting, 1995 & 2000.

Eckman, Paul, *Why Kids Lie,* Penguin Books, 1991.

Fleming, Don, *How to stop battling with your child,* Prentice Hall, 1993 and *How to stop battling with your Teenager,* Prentice Hall, 1993.

Gray, Dr. John, *Mars & Venus; Starting Over,* Harper Collins, 2007.

Gordon, Dr. Tomas, *Parent effectiveness training; Proven program for raising responsible children,* Random House, 2001.

Greer, Dr Jane, *What about me? Stop Selfishness from ruining your relationship,* Sourcebooks Inc, 2010.

Killinger, Barbara, *Workaholics; The respectable Addicts,* Key Porter Books, Toronto, 2004.

Rapoport, Judith, *The Boy Who Couldn't Stop Washing,* Penguin Books, 1999.

Tannen, Deborah, *You Just Don't Understand; Women and Men in Conversation,* Harper Collins, 2007.

Uly, William, *Getting Past No; Negotiating with Difficult People,* Random House, 2002.

Woititz, Dr. Janet G., *The Intimacy Struggle,* Health Communications, 1993.

Wylie, Betty Jane, *Beginnings; A book for widows,* McClelland & Stewart, 1997.

Made in the USA
Coppell, TX
29 August 2020